MY SELF,
MY MANY SELVES

THE LIBRARY OF ANALYTICAL PSYCHOLOGY
VOLUME VI

MY SELF, MY MANY SELVES

Joseph W. T. Redfearn

Routledge
Taylor & Francis Group
LONDON AND NEW YORK

First published 1985 by Academic Press Inc. London

This edition 1994 published by
Karnac Books Ltd.

Published 2018 by Routledge
2 Park Square, Milton Park, Abingdon, Oxon OX14 4RN
711 Third Avenue, New York, NY 10017, USA

Routledge is an imprint of the Taylor & Francis Group, an informa business

British Library Cataloguing in Publication Data
A C.I.P. for this book is available from the British Library

ISBN 9781855750821 (pbk)

Contents

Foreword

The concept of the "self" has remained puzzling and controversial. Indeed, far from gaining in clarity, it seems to become ever more complex; for many different people, starting from different premises and having different goals have come to "appropriate" this term.

Joe Redfearn has made what seems to me to be a most valuable contribution by sticking firmly to an experiential approach. He has thought hard and deeply about the different ways in which we experience the "I" and drawn on his own "I" experience as well as on those of his patients and of Jung himself.

He tells us in his introduction that the main aim of his book is to illustrate the migratory nature of the feeling of "I" and that the goal of analysis is to "facilitate and open up interaction and inter-communication between our various selves".

The origin of these many and varied selves tends to be named differently according to the school or discipline involved as, for instance, "archetype", "complex", "internal object", "part-object", "introjected environmental personage", "part of body-image", "part-brain function" etc. In order to facilitate true observation and inter-communication, Joe Redfearn has given these different selves a generic, descriptive name; thinking of them as actors in a play he calls them "sub-personalities". This name enables us to speak to one another and know what we mean whatever our school or discipline, and yet we are left free to continue our search or research for the possible origin or roots of these sub-personalities.

It must be clear from what he has defined as his main aim that Joe Redfearn values actual and personal experience and unbiased and unprejudged observation of it above partial or premature abstraction. Yet his grasp of abstraction and theory is masterly. His first chapter on "Ego and self" in which he discusses these terms as used by the principal psychoanalysts and analytical psychologists is invaluable as a guide through the various theoretical formulations, definitions and developmental schemas.

Joe Redfearn is generous in the way he allows the reader to see into those of his own life experiences which became the source and cradle of his present-day views and understanding. Many came, of course, from his experience of, and his work with, his patients, and this book is packed with descriptions of them; he uses them liberally as examples, and it is clear that for Joe Redfearn analysands are not only his patients, they are also his teachers.

One of the factors that attracted me to the Jungian school was that I seemed to find there a relatively open system of theories, that is, a schema relatively unencumbered by dogmatic beliefs and premature conclusions. I had sought for space, both for individuality of different patients and for freedom of work and discoveries of future researchers.

I believe it was this openness that also drew Joe Redfearn to analytical psychology. Whether my assumption is correct or not, here is a colleague firmly grounded in Jungian theory, yet able to observe and report freely and sensitively over a wide field of human behaviour, endeavour, phantasy and experience. This is a most gratifying testimony to the research-potential inherent in and encouraged by our particular school.

The book is written beautifully, with a fine sense for poetry, an almost deceptive clarity and an obvious aversion for the facile, the pretentious and the pompous.

As in all the previous volumes of the Library of Analytical Psychology, all references to Jung's writings are taken from the Collected Works, abbreviated *Coll. Wks*, followed by the volume number. The dates refer to the first publication in whatever language and not to the English translation.

Rosemary Gordon

Preface

My way of working is a product of the London Society of Analytical Psychology; my own analysis, supervision, the seminars, the discussion groups with colleagues about our work, the hundreds of sessions with colleagues, particularly those in the Society's working party on training during my twelve years as Director of Training (Adult) for the Society, have been the main factors moulding my particular approach to analysis.

Because of the constant support of my colleagues, friends and people I love, I have been able to keep up a modest though steady flow of writing over the years. My wife has shown a great deal of forbearance during those periods of irritable snappiness and withdrawal when I have been in the throes of what I subjectively experience as creative suffering or suffering creativity – regardless of the objective value of what eventually is borne out of it.

This book represents a thorough revision of views expressed in some of my earlier papers, with much that is spelled out here clearly for the first time. The notion of sub-personalities and of the migratory feeling of "I", for example, is one which has dominated my clinical work for many years but which I have not anywhere adumbrated at all fully before. I am grateful to the Editor of *The Journal of Analytical Psychology* for allowing me to use material from my articles in the Journal as a basis for Chapters 1, 2, 4, 6 and 7, and to the Editor of the *British Journal of Medical Psychology* for allowing me to use material from an article of mine in that Journal which is the foundation of Chapter 5.

I am especially grateful to Kenneth Lambert and the other Editors of this series of books for encouraging me to produce this volume. Kenneth Lambert put in a lot of work in the formative stages and later. Rosemary Gordon has been of immense help not only in providing support and ideas in the earlier stages but also in helping me to revise and rewrite later drafts, when the initial creative enthusiasm had flagged and it was an effort to confront the results of one's labours yet again.

The findings described herein are largely the result of 25 years of work as a practising analyst. Finally and most of all, I wish to express my gratitude to the analysands throughout these years who have worked with me, making my work so richly rewarding.

Joseph Redfearn

Introduction

"Is anyone there?" asks Pooh Bear in A. A. Milne's classic book, when he comes across the hole of his friend Rabbit while wandering in the forest. To Pooh, this means two things: honey and someone who will listen to the new tune he has just made up.

In response there is only a frightened scuffling within. Rabbit fears danger. Pooh has to try again. "Is anyone at home?" Then the exchange proceeds as follows:

> "No"
> "Isn't that Rabbit?"
> "No. At least it's not supposed to be."
> "Where is he, then?"
> "He's gone to visit his very good friend Pooh Bear"
> "But that's me."
> "What sort of a me is that?"
> "Pooh Bear"
> "Well, that's all right then."

Evidently the establishment of personal identity is a matter for negotiation. The particular identities established are a function of the purpose in hand.

I do not wish to trouble the reader by asking him this question (Is anyone there?) out of the blue. I have no wish to send him scurrying for cover. I hope we shall get along pretty well without thrusting such questions at anybody. Suppose I asked myself "Who am I?", while rushing upstairs or, even worse, downstairs. Many a person has come a nasty cropper in that way. Such a rumination at such a time might surely represent a transaction between two personalities within oneself who were not relating at all comfortably with each other.

In this book I am concerned with the "I" and the "self" mainly as experience. Yet one must admit that the experience of "I" or of "myself" is usually absent or in the background when life is going on normally. Even so, without our being aware of it, the feeling of "I" may be taken over first by a hungry Pooh within us, then by a fearful Rabbit and so on. There is a seemingly endless parade of sub-personalities within our total personality, all ready to take the stage and play their allotted roles.

If one of these possible characters within us is denied his rightful prominence in the drama which is ourself he may stage a take-over or irruption. In Chapter 3, I give what I believe to be an example of this, using my own life story as a case in point. In this example, one could say that "God" (or an infantile-omnipotent sub-personality, depending on one's point of view), having been somewhat left out of my "I", invaded my subjective self in a "religious" experience of a fairly typical sort. In other chapters, there are examples of other sub-personalities asserting themselves. Sometimes we can demonstrate take-over by ego-alien forces of the part of the body (body-image more precisely) where the "I" is located (see Chapter 6).

This book does not deal in detail with the way in which healthy self-feeling or background-identity is normally acquired in the interaction between infant and mother and between the child and important others. I regard the work of Freud, Jung, Erikson, Winnicott, Kohut and many others as basic reading and I have not attempted a summary or critique of it all.

If the "I" is not allowed free range over the repertoire of possible roles, tension or imbalance may result. We all have preferred self-images, which amount to defensive systems aimed at keeping at bay parts of ourselves we do not wish to be. I try to show in the last two chapters that it is these defences which prevent our reaching our own cherished goals and our "self-realization". For what is being kept out and defended against is a needy, invasive, hostile or deprived self who can never break through to what it wants (being prevented from doing so by these very defences).

From the point of the questing "I", the relatively inaccessible self represents both the highest goal and the deepest regression. The defences of the self and the need for security are the basis both for the quest of self-fulfilment and for the obstacles in its own path.

One of the main aims of this book is to illustrate the migratory nature of the feeling of "I". This "I" migrates hither and thither to various locations in the total personality, like the spotlight at a theatre picking out first one actor then another, or, even more pertinently, like a pilgrim on his journey of life visiting one place, then another, in his universe. What are these basic units of personality, each of which may take the stage and relate to other units in sometimes familiar, sometimes novel dramas and stories? I call these various actors in ourselves "sub-personalities", because I think a generic, not too controversial word is necessary at this stage in the working concepts which psychotherapists use.

The reason for a generic term is so that we can get on with observing and intercommunicating about ourselves and our patients. Using terms which assume "knowledge" which is partial or controversial may prevent this. What are these sub-personalities called and what is their origin? Various schools of psychotherapy answer this question – prematurely in my opinion – in ways which simply conflict because they each stress one origin for sub-personalities at the expense of others. Jungians speak of "archetypes" and "complexes" as basic units. Freudians use units such as ego, id and introjected aspects of mother, father and so on ("internalized objects"). In clinical practice it is usually impossible, even after prolonged analysis, to decide how much a given sub-personality (occurring repeatedly, as they do, in dreams and changing gradually in the course of analysis) originates innately and how much it is an introjected "environmental object". The question of "how much" it is one and "how much" the other is meaningless in this form anyhow.

Speaking off-hand, the following list of origins occurs to me in contributing to our sub-personalities, the many "selves" referred to in the title of this book.

(1) Archetypes.
(2) Complexes.
(3) Introjected "objects" (parental images etc.).
(4) Introjected "part objects" (Kleinian terminology).
(5) Parts of the "body-image", or bodily functions, may function as sub-personalities.
(6) Part-brain functions may function in this way. For example, in a patient whose cerebral hemispheres are not properly connected with each other, the left side may function as an alien sub-personality. There is every reason to suppose that various degrees of block of a similar sort could happen in our normal selves.
(7) Deities and social values, social ideals.

These categories of sub-personality overlap. Each category has been studied by different schools and disciplines.

I do not wish of course to interfere with the work of any of these schools and disciplines, nor do I wish to prevent Jungians from talking about archetypes or Freudians from talking about father-figures etc. But I do feel that a generic term is indicated especially in psychotherapy, when we do not wish to pretend that we know the exact nature or origin of a given sub-personality. The term might lessen the irritation and confusion which tends to occur when Jungians, Freudians, transactional analysts, biodynamic therapists and Gestalt therapists attempt to communicate with each other.

Michael Fordham, who was my analyst and who contributed much to the ideas and practice of the "London" school of Jungians to which I belong, speaks about "de-integration" and "de-integrates" when describing these various part-selves. I am not sure how far my "sub-personalities" include his "de-integrates" but I feel that they are not at all identical concepts and that, even if identical, the word "sub-personality" is more descriptive and closer to the observed ways in which these units behave.

The ways in which sub-personalities interact (usually in mental activity or in outward behaviour) are of course legion and if we take the theatre analogy would correspond to the sum total of possible plots and scenarios which are infinite in number but which nevertheless tend to follow certain well-known and well-loved patterns. Therefore, we could possibly talk about the "enantiodroma" of the sub-personalities using a word that Jung often used in a similar sense. In this book I do not deal with these common motifs or themes of dynamic interaction which are of the essence of the relationships concerned. For the relatively universal themes of myths, legends, stories and historical patterns we can obviously use the term "archetypal themes" or "archetypal motifs". It is only for a more general term corresponding to the more general concept of "sub-personality" as opposed to "archetype" that we at present do not have a ready candidate. "Enantiodroma of sub-personalities" is hardly a phrase that could be advocated on account of its musical qualities. But never mind about that for the moment. Why should one worry about finding a phrase for a concept that at the moment interests no one but oneself?

The first chapter of this book is intended to show that some of the confusion among analysts in this field is due to unacknowledged differences in terminological usage. It will gradually become evident that not all the confusion is terminological, but that "feeling of I", "self-concept" (or self representation) and "total personality" are inextricably interwoven concepts (images, feelings, experiences or whatever). Nevertheless it seems to me a worthwhile exercise to separate terminological confusion from more fundamental, psychological difficulties and "mysteries".

Chapter One

Ego and self: terminology

Introduction

A psychological schema of the structure of the mind is like a map. It should not be confused with the real thing. A map is used for a purpose. A geological map would be useless to a motorist. A sociologist's map would be different from a psychotherapist's. Freudian, Jungian and behavioural psychotherapists need different maps because of their differing goals and methods of arriving at them.

I said that the map should not be confused with the real thing. What is the "real thing" in the case of the mind? A series of maps or representations? If so, what is the nature of the "I" to whom they are presented? A further series of representations? Is the "I" based on energy/matter, or is energy/matter merely a split-off, ephemeral and alienated aspect of a universal "I" or psyche? Or can we arrive at our personal resolution of these apparently polarized views of the nature of the psyche and of matter?

How far does introspection lead us in our experience of ourself? Our experience of ourselves is necessarily a matter for introspection, if not for introspection alone. Writing in 1910, Williams James distinguished between "I", the self as knower and doer, and "me", or myself as known or experienced. He saw no value in studying the "I" as a knower and felt it should be banished to the realms of philosophy. Concerning the "myself" as known, James included a material self which contained one's body, one's family and one's possessions; then a social self which was a reflection of the way other people see the individual; and finally a spiritual self which included emotions and desires.

All these aspects of the self have stood the test of time and have been studied in detail. Furthermore, James recognized that all these aspects of self were capable of evoking feelings of heightened or lowered self-esteem. And finally, James described the self as carrying a feeling of basic unity and continuity, even while being highly differentiated.

Cooley (1912) defined "self" as that which is designated in common speech by the pronouns of the first person singular – I, me, mine, myself. The self is characterized by stronger emotions than is the non-self. Cooley introduced the concept of the "looking-glass self" – the individual perceiving himself in the way others see him. Taking this idea further, George Mead (1934) argued that the self-concept in fact arises out of the individual's concern about how others react to him. Mead hypothesized a "generalized other" to account for generalized feelings about oneself. He averred that there are as many selves as there are social roles played by an individual. H. S. Sullivan (1953) agreed but stressed the importance of the mother as the most significant other person in determining the self-concept.

Allport (1955) used the word "proprium" to include the following attributes:

(1) Awareness of a bodily self.
(2) Sense of a continuity over time.
(3) A need for self-esteem.
(4) An extension of the "I" or ego beyond the borders of the body.
(5) An ability to synthesize inner needs and outer reality.
(6) A self-image, a perception and evaluation of the self as an object of knowledge.
(7) There is the self as *knower* and *doer*.
(8) There is on occasions a need to increase tensions, expand awareness, seek and meet challenges etc.

I mention these authors in the general psychological literature because their contributions seem to me basically sound and fundamental ones.

Ego and Self in Psychoanalysis

In attempting to sketch developments in psychoanalytic terminology, I shall need to shorten and over-simplify to such a degree as perhaps to cause pain to each reader. I shall need much generosity from all, as each would summarize important changes in his own way. But I am not writing about the authors' actual views. I am using selected quotations and summaries in order to discuss terminology, typical possible terminologies. I might have invented the quotations myself without affecting the validity of this chapter, which is written to alert the reader to terminological confusions. The scope for confusion is not limited to terminology, and some readers will be offended by the simplistic clarity of my presentation, which in a sense ignores the real, non-terminological confusions and paradoxes in the actual phenomenology of the experiences described below.

Freud

In abandoning hypnosis in the therapy of neurosis, Freud discovered resistance and laid the foundation of psychoanalysis. At first his "ego" was roughly equivalent to the conscious and preconscious parts of the mind. The unconscious, on the other hand, contained repressed contents. Libido was the expression of the sexual instinct, with the ego in conflict, responsible for repression and reality-testing. In his early papers, Freud regarded the ego as the organ of defence, but even in 1896 he knew that some defences are unconscious. The term "das Ich" was also used sometimes to distinguish oneself as a whole from other people. Strachey says that when he meets this use, he usually translates it as "the self" (Freud, 1923 *Std Edn*, **19**, 7).

By 1914–15 Freud was distinguishing between ego instincts and object instincts. In this context ego means oneself. Megalomania was explained in terms of these ego instincts, as were self-regard and self-esteem.

In his essay "On narcissism", written about that time, Freud (1914) described the antithesis between ego-libido and object-libido. He used the simile of an amoeba throwing out pseudopods, suggesting a basic unity of libido but flowing in opposite directions.

By this time Freud is beginning to develop the idea of a super-ego comparing the behaviour of the individual with that of his ego-ideal. He used the notion to explain the paraphrenic's delusions of being watched. He saw the primary state of the infant as that of boundaryless self-love which he called primary narcissism, but self and not-self were as yet undifferentiated. He saw the ego developing out of this state by displacement of libido on to the mother and later on to an ideal. Satisfaction is brought about by fulfilling the mother's (later the ideal's) requirements.

Later, Freud used this interplay between object libido and narcissism to account for the building-up of complex functions, such as sublimation and the fusion or neutralization of instincts.

In his important paper "The ego and the id" Freud (1923) made his last theoretic reformulation of the structure of the mind. He distinguished carefully between ego and the quality of consciousness, and he elaborated the watching faculty of the super-ego, taken to pathological extremes in obsessional neurosis and pathological mourning. The super-ego is held to arise out of the transformation of oedipal object cathexis into identifications, and takes the place of the Oedipus complex. Freud restricted the term "unconscious" to that which has been repressed. He now defined the ego as a coherent organization of mental processes. It is to this ego that consciousness is attached. It controls the approaches to motility and goes to sleep at night. Even then it censors the dreams. It is responsible for repressions and resistances. But resistances, although emanating from the ego, are unconscious. So part of the ego is unconscious, and "behaves exactly like the repressed" in producing powerful effects. Now he derives neuroses not from a conflict between conscious and unconscious, but between the coherent ego and the repressed which is split off from it.

An unconscious thought becomes conscious, via the preconscious, by becoming connected with word-presentations, which are residues of memories. Consciousness is primarily to do with this system of word-presentation. Internal perceptions (from internal sensory apparatus) become conscious directly, bypassing the preconscious, when they become conscious at all.

The other part of the mind, into which the ego extends, was now called the "id", following Groddeck, who regarded the ego as a surface phenomenon merely being lived out by the unconscious forces of the id. Part of the lower ego is discontinuous with the id owing to repression. Thus the ego is that part of the id which has been modified by the direct influence of the external world through the medium of perceptions; it is in a sense an extension of the surface-differentiation. The ego mediates between the instincts and the external world through the reality principle and not through self-regard. Freud described the ego in its relations to the id as like a man on horseback. Often, he says, the man has to guide the horse where it wants to go. The ego is first and foremost a body ego, ultimately derived from bodily sensations, and itself the projection of the bodily surface. The reservoir of libido is now clearly the id. In later writings Freud used the concept of an undifferentiated ego–id forming a great reservoir of libido.

A large body of psychoanalytic literature has arisen surrounding "ego-defences" and "ego-boundaries". In her book *The Ego and the Mechanisms of Defence*, Anna Freud (1946) elaborates on the defences used by the ego to defend the ego. Here she is often referring to the feeling of "I" or "myself" and not merely to the system "ego" as defined above by Freud. The notion of ego-boundaries and their preservation also refers to the self as distinct from others and not to Freud's system ego.

Klein, Winnicott and Erikson

The psychoanalysis of children and of psychotic patients has enriched our knowledge of early and archaic levels of the development of personal identity. One thinks of such analysts as Melanie Klein, Erikson and Winnicott as making fundamental contributions to terminology.

Melanie Klein uses the term "ego" to mean both the subjective "I" or "myself" on the one hand, and the "system ego" on the other, with its various stage-appropriate ways of enhancing, depending and strengthening itself. Just as the baby sucks, takes in, shrinks from, spits out and eliminates various objects in his struggle to survive, so the infant ego is seen taking in, avoiding spitting out and eliminating good and bad "objects" or parts of "objects" (mental representations of bits of his environment). Thus the ego arises out of some sort of mental representation ("brain map") of the baby himself. This is not nonsense, as would first appear, because the baby himself, his insides, his outside and the world of vision and hearing give rise to nervous impulses which are topographically distributed throughout the nervous system. Thus the body-image as sensed and perceived is an accurate map, in his brain, of the baby himself. The Kleinian views the ego and the psyche as a body-ego and a psyche-ego. The Kleinian "mechanisms" are all derived from as well as representations of bodily processes, sensations and reactions.

In his classic work *Childhood and Society* and his other writings, Erikson (1950), while adhering in his definition of ego to Freud's definition, writes of ego identity and of the growth of a personal sense of identity. He writes of the ego as if it were a kind of person dwelling between the extremes of the "bestial" impersonal id and the conscience which is often harsh and restrictive. The ego keeps tuned to reality and integrates the individual's planning and orientation. Admittedly it uses "defence mechanisms", but "we wish to extend our reach beyond the mere defensive aspects". The ego is an "inner institution", evolved to safeguard order within the individual. In the case of a schizophrenic girl, "we see a very young ego struggle for coherence, and fail". Play situations "indicate the narrow area within which our ego can feel superior to the confinement of space and time and to the definitiveness of social reality – free from the compulsions of conscience and from impulsions of irrationality." Here the ego is clearly a self with human feelings, closely related to well-being and good self-esteem. In this book, Erikson describes the child's acquisition of a sound sense of personal identity based on the body image, and goes on to trace this development in the adult. He thus extends the concept of the "I" to that of a personal identity and gives descriptions of clinical aspects of "ego-growth" and of failures in this area. For Erikson this personal identity has primarily a mediating function between inner and outer needs, between instincts and standards, etc.

Winnicott (1965), on the other hand, uses the term "ego" to mean an integrating function of the brain present from the beginning. Thus an anencephalic infant would have an id but no ego, whereas an infant with a normal brain would already have an ego as well as an id. The ego is there from the start. In fact "the start is when the ego starts". "It will be seen", says Winnicott (1965), "that the ego offers itself for study long before the word self has relevance." "The word self arrives after the child has begun to use the intellect to look at what others see or feel or hear and what they conceive of when they meet this infant body." "The strength of the ego depends on the actual mother's ability to meet the absolute dependence of the actual infant at the beginning, at the stage before the infant has separated out the mother from the self." It is possible "to violate the infant's ego-function, or that which later on will be jealously guarded as the self, the core of the personality" if the mother lacks the capacity to protect the infant from unthinkable anxiety by being able to put herself in the baby's place and know what the baby needs in the general management of the body and therefore of the person.

A baby is a person who is on the brink of unthinkable anxiety which has the following varieties:

(1) Going to pieces.
(2) Falling for ever.
(3) Having no relationship to the body.
(4) Having no orientation.

These anxieties are the stuff of psychotic anxieties. What is threatened is what Winnicott terms ego-functioning or, subjectively, what will only later become the self in his terminology. Maternal failure at this stage can lead to schizoid disorder and to the formation of a false self which is an attempt at self-holding.

For Winnicott, ego development depends on the ego-supportive mother and is characterized by the following trends:

(1) integration in time and space, depending on the mother's *holding*.
(2) Personalization – the development of the body ego and of a firm union of ego and body, depending on the mother's *handling*.
(3) Object-relating, both to things and persons, depending on the mother's way and timing of *object-presentation*.

Differentiation into "I" and "you", into "I" and "non-I", the development of subjective objects and of objectively experienced objects, and of his capacity for realism proceeds gradually so long as the mother understands the child's reality limitations. For a long time the child retains areas of subjective objects as well as areas of objectively perceived objects ("not-me" objects).

Thus in Winnicott's rather comprehensive terminology, the ego is the original integrating function; schizoid mechanisms arise out of threats to the pre-self (or what will later become the self) and the self is oneself as distinct from other people, and is importantly dependent on how others experience the individual. In other words, it is a function of reflection from others. Thus the self for Winnicott is what arises out of the differentiation of an original integrate.

Jacobson, Hartmann, Fordham and Kohut

For Edith Jacobson (1964), in her book *The Self and the Object World*, and for Michael Fordham (1976) in his book *The Self and Autism* the original integrate is called "the primal self". For Jacobson (1964, p. 19) "the establishment of the system ego sets in with the discovery of the object world and the growing distinction between it and one's own physical and mental self". Jacobson's terminology is thus more or less the opposite of Winnicott's as far as ego and self are concerned. For Fordham also the ego is related to the experience of "I" and is differentiated out of the primal self; it is only a part of the whole self. However, neither Jacobson nor Fordham are consistent in their use of the word "self". For example, Jacobson's use of the word self in the sentence just quoted ("one's own physical and mental self" as distinct from the "not-me") does not conform with her own definition of her use of the word "self", and coincides with Winnicott's self. And Fordham (1974) describes some schizoid defences as defences of the self when he is not speaking of the primary integrate or total personality but of a pre-"myself", or pre-ego in Jungian terminology.

Jacobson states that her definition of "self" is based on Hartmann's (1950) definition as the whole individual, including mind and body. Jacobson (1964, p. 6) says that the term self was introduced by Hartmann, and thus she ignores the voluminous writings on the subject by C. G. Jung, on whose work Fordham's definition and concepts are based.

Hartmann certainly pioneered a major trend in psychoanalytic theory, and made clear distinction between "ego" and "self". For Hartmann (e.g. Hartmann, 1964) the ego is not defined in terms of self-feeling, the experience of "I" or any other subjective experience or subjectively experienced datum, but as a system of adaptive and integrative functions hierarchically arranged. Functions of defence and anti-instinctual aspects are included in the functions of the ego. Adaptation to "reality" is the main emphasis, a biological view. Obviously some of those ego functions would be present from the beginning of the individual, and so Hartmann's definition of ego is similar to Winnicott's.

Hartmann also defines the self in much the same way as does Winnicott. It is very much to do with feelings and subjective experience and with the distinction between myself and not-me. For example (Hartmann, 1964, p. 127), he says "It will therefore be clarifying if we define narcissism as the libidinal cathexis not of the ego but of the self." He thus diverges considerably in his terminology from the early and middle Freud, while not of course ignoring any of Freud's findings or basic ideas. In his ego functions Hartmann includes reality-orientated, anti-instinctual functions such as the postponement of gratification and the neutralization of instincts, and generally adheres to the post-1923 Freudian view of psychic structure. But differentiation of "ego" from "self" no doubt helped later psychoanalysts such as Jacobson and especially Heinz Kohut in their clinical work on narcissism and narcissistic disorders.

Kohut (1971, p. xiii) pays tribute to Hartmann's conceptual separation of the self from the ego, in paving the way to his work on identity and on the subjective self which is clinically of such importance. He points out that the self in his terminology is to do with the representation of the self in the psyche analogous to the representations of other persons and things in the psyche ("object-representations"). He uses the description "experience-near" of this concept of the self, whereas the term "ego" is used as an abstract concept describing or defining a psychic system. Much of the basic fabric of this ego, for Kohut, consists of introjections of the approving and disapproving aspects of the pre-oedipal mother. (I personally would agree and would add that many of the holding and containing aspects of the ego are introjected from early experience of the mother in the same way.) With Freud, Kohut derives the super-ego from introjections of the "post-oedipal object" (the post-oedipal mother and father).

Kohut's work on narcissism and his use of the "self" to mean the object of narcissistic libido are making it more and more difficult to use the word self in the way Jung used it, without using some such terms as Greater Self, or whole personality, or Jungian self or self with a capital S to distinguish this Jungian self from Kohut's self. The latter approximates to Jung's "ego". The later writings of Kohut encompass to some degree the Jungian self, but a detailed discussion of this would be out of place here.

It could be asserted that as the individual person matures, the self in the sense of the object of narcissistic libido, the ego in the sense of mediating and containing functions, the sense of personal identity and the Jungian self all tend more and more to overlap or coincide. We see the late Kohut grappling with these real (non-terminological) issues, just as Jung did in his writings about ego and self.

Jung, Neumann and Fordham

Jung used the word "self" to describe (at various times) (see Redfearn, 1977):

(1) A primary cosmic unity analogous to oriental concepts of the unity of oneself and all creatures and things.
(2) The totality of the individual.
(3) The experience of or intimation of such a totality, an experience of "wholeness".
(4) A primary organizing force or agency outside the conscious "I".
(5) The unconscious or the organizing centre of the unconscious.
(6) Emerging part of the self.

For Jung, the term "self" is used for a totality or for a mainly "not-me" force in or centre of the psyche which is usually not experienced clearly by the conscious "I". Jung's "self" is placed over against his "ego", which corresponds with Freud's pre-1914 ego. This is not surprising as the divergence between Freud and Jung dated from about 1913. Of course, in its aspect of the total personality, Jung's "self" would include "ego", so that thus defined it would consist of "ego plus unconscious" or "ego plus archetypes", but Jung does not always use the term in this way. The self is for Jung not something experienced directly, but, as in the Platonic and neo-Platonic tradition, indirectly through symbols, stories and numerous experiences including religious experiences.

Jung does not distinguish in his use of the term "ego" between the subjective "I" and the functions of defence and adaptation described later by Anna Freud and Hartmann. His "ego" is very much akin to Kohut's "self" in that it is generally *experience-near*, that is near to the experience or feeling of "I", "me", "myself", my "identity". Indeed, Jung often defines it as a centre of awareness or of consciousness. Somewhat paradoxically, perhaps, he regards the ego as a sort of complex. Complexes, which were Jung's own discovery, are largely unconscious, like sub-personalities or sub-selves affecting consciousness and behaviour but avoiding direct relationship with the "I". Jung's "ego" is an integrating and organizing force (in *that* it does not differ from other "complexes") and both the organizing function and the subjective unity of the "I" may become fragmented, as in schizophrenia. "Therefore, with a schizophrenic, you often see a rapid change from one personality to another" (Jung, 1935, p. 12). This looseness of the "I" in its attachment to the various sub-personalities of the individual, resulting in a readier migration of "I-feeling" between the different sub-personalities, also characterizes the dream-ego in comparison with the normal waking-ego (Hall, 1982). In the same lecture, Jung (1935) defines the ego as "a complex datum of experience which is constituted first of all by a general awareness of your body, of your existence, and secondly by your memory data" (continuity in space and time). Thus Jung's "ego" is similar to Winnicott's "self" and to the Hartmann–Kohut "self". Jung's "ego", like Hartmann's "self", is the object of one's self-esteem, self-awareness, self-value etc.; Jung's ego is also the active, willing, doing "I". "Will", for Jung, is determined by the amount of libido at the disposal of the ego, which in this context is active, doing and very much the subject and not the object. It is hardly necessary to describe the development of Jung's views of the ego, because they hardly vary throughout his writings in these essential respects. His concepts of the "self" and "individuation", however, developed after about 1911, and were very much a result of personal experience and of the influence of philosophy, religion and personal anguish.

Freud's "sub-personalities" (my term), his ego, id and super-ego all behave as though they are integrative, organizing centres of our personalities, almost as if they are people or daemons within us, partly conscious, largely rooted in the unconscious, first one taking charge of the "I", or of behaviour or both, then the other.

Jung's sub-personalities, the ego, the persona, the shadow, the anima, the wise man, the wise woman, the self etc., as well as the complexes, behave as organizing centres and each may take charge in turn of the feelings of "I" and of behaviour. They all have an innate basis and yet all are influenced by experience and they all differentiate through experience. Thus the ego (Jung, 1950b, p. 5) is acquired in the individual's lifetime and arises from the interaction of body and environment. The shadow also is partly acquired during one's lifetime (consisting of negative introjects – author's term) and yet has an innate foundation – like absolute evil. Thus archetypes and even more complexes contain positive and negative introjected elements, yet – and this is the innate element – one can only introject what one *is* in the first place, in an important sense.

The term introjection is a question-begging one in that it assumes that one is incorporating into the personality something that is outside the personality, or incorporating into the "myself" something that is originally experienced as "not-myself". For example, I may say that the infant tends to "introject" the mother's affirming and the mother's rejecting attitudes respectively towards different behaviours (termed "good" and "bad" respectively by the mother). But the infant can only incorporate the mother's attitudes in so far as it is capable of having these attitudes. It will incorporate his own version or his own experience of these attitudes, and what he "incorporates" will be essentially what he himself is and what he is "projecting" on to the mother.

What *is* important are the positive and negative feeling-tones which are introjected. These feelings are incorporated into the personality as positive and negative inter-relationships between the various sub-personalities in oneself.

Let us take such negative behaviours and attitudes as "I despise . . .", "I am terrified of . . .", "I ignore . . .", "I turn my back on . . ." etc. All these are primary attitudes or behaviours needed originally for self-protection. If my mother has these attitudes towards various bits of myself, then what I end up with is a situation in which a "mother" bit of myself is negatively related to a "child" bit of myself. The concept of shadow is vague and generalized in clinical practice. In clinical practice we need to know about the part of the personality which is disapproving, the part disapproved of, and the specific nature (disgust, contempt, denial, fear etc.) of the negative interaction.

It is easy to see that it is the negative attitudes rather than the affirming ones which when introjected give rise to complexes, fixations, repressions, resistances etc., because the "I" is usually identified with the original rejector (the on-the-whole loved or good mother, the on-the-whole accepted values of society etc).

Just as Jung remained consistent in speaking of the self more as the whole personality and the ego as the "I" linked with self-valuation and the sense of personal identity, so later analytical psychologists have consistently maintained these broad definitions. However, an important Jungian variation on this theme sees the self, or at any rate the way the self presents itself to consciousness, as an organizing centre essentially based in the unconscious, only partly capable of being perceived directly in consciousness. Thus the inner voice, the God image, the Christ figure, the treasure beyond price, the philosopher's stone, the Grail etc. have all been taken as symbols or symbolic experiences through which the conscious ego puts itself in touch with, or is put in touch with, these unconscious forces. Writing recently in *The Journal of Analytical Psychology*, Humbert (1980) says "If you were to ask what the self signifies for me, I should reply that it is, above all, the inner voice which tells me frequently and precisely how I am to live." One should observe, I believe, that Humbert's inner voice has some of the qualities of a French parent. But no Jungian analyst would maintain that the inner voice was *merely* the introjected parental voice. As I have just said, one can only introject that which one already *is* in a sense.

It must be stated here that these so-called symbols of the self, the inner voice, the image of God etc. are not usually experienced as part of one's own personality or as part of oneself, but are usually experienced as coming from the "not-me". This has left Jungians open to the charge of mysticism, levelled at them by some psychoanalysts. To speak of God, or of the God image at least, as a self-image or self-symbol, even as a symbol of the totality of the psyche, seems to beg all sorts of philosophical and theological questions. But from the empirical psychological point of view, we take these images and symbols as products of the psyche. This in turn seems to lead us to a view of the psyche as having no specific location in relation to the subjective "me". Or, to put it another way, the "I" may at different times be located in differing parts or locations within the total universe of the self. Some theologians might assert that God "exists" not only "out there", but at the deepest core of one's being, without, nowadays, being accused of being mystical. Jung, much more than Freud, always insisted that the unconscious parts of the self (of the total personality that is) are experienced "in projection", that is they are experienced as outside the subjective "me", in other people for example. And moreover, that they must be faced, or "worked-through", in the moral conflicts of real relationships.

Another source of confusion for Jungian analysts and writers is the actual images which are used by the psyche to symbolize the harmonizing and organizing aspects of the psyche, or the wholeness of the personality. They are felt by the individual to represent the whole, especially if they are numinous symbols or experiences. I am speaking of the mandalas and of "divine" images existing in the religions of mankind which Jung experienced in himself and in his patients, and which Fordham and others have shown to be produced in children and to be related often to the emergence of a sense of personal identity (see Fordham, 1969). In other words, these images often seem subjectively to be numinous images signifying a Greater Whole, whereas to the outside observer these images, in their personal aspects and defensive functions and so on, are very much to do with the individual's need to *feel* whole or secure. The more unaware or regressed a person is, the more the various sub-personalities and complexes comprising his total personality are successively experienced by him as the whole thing – the whole truth, the whole of himself, the will of God, ultimate good etc. In other words, parts of the total personality take over the feeling of "myself" and seem like the whole of the self or even of the cosmos. To the outside observer the individual may simply be in a "possessed" or regressed state. To take a theatrical analogy, it is as if different actors successively occupy the whole stage, each thinking he is the whole show, whereas the audience (the analyst) knows that each is only part of the evening's performance.

Thus the various Jungian "symbols of the self" are themselves only parts of the personality, or represent, objectively, only parts of the total personality. Yet subjectively, and even objectively, they may point towards a greater harmony or wholeness and lead or inspire the individual towards further integrations and self-awareness.

From the therapeutic point of view it is often valuable to say to the patient "That image (dream image, drawing, painting, character in a play) is *you*." This helps him expand his awareness of hitherto unconscious, acted-out or projected, parts of his personality not at present experienced as "me" or as part of the "myself".

Apart from giving rise to symbolic experiences, a "sub-personality" or "part-self" may carry the feeling of "myself" at times, or it may possess the individual behaviourally and be acted out relatively unawares. The third main method of discharge is through projection on to others.

Psychoanalysts of all schools describe the development of personality in terms of an emergence of a separate identity from a state of dependence and subjective non-differentiation from one's environment. In Erikson's terms, this is the development of personal identity, in Winnicott's it is the growth of the separate self out of the primal state of ego-functioning. Jungians tend to speak as the emergence of the "ego" out of the primal matrix as both ego and not-ego become more differentiated. The analytical psychologist Erich Neumann (1954) sees the myths of mankind mainly as the story of this struggle of the (Jungian) "ego" to free itself from the unconscious – the state of primitive or unaware non-differentiation or boundarylessness. As the ego (the hero figure of myths and other stories) becomes free and well-established, the various unconscious sub-personalities (archetypes and complexes) evolve alongside and differentiate, and become in general less monstrous and more human. Thus, both "I" and "not-I" evolve and differentiate together with each other in a constant dynamic, dramatized in the great religions and myths of mankind. Neumann (1954) refers to this process of ego-development and the consequent changes in the way the ego relates to the unconscious and to other people as the emergence of ego-consciousness from the primordial matrix. As each successive stage is laboriously attained, the stage just relinquished becomes a fascinating devourer, a temptation, a sin etc.

In his paper "The self as an imaginative construct", Fordham (1979) examines in some detail the groups of experience which may carry the feeling of being "myself". He calls these groups of experience "part selves" and these are similar to what I am here calling "sub-personalities". He includes archetypes such as the individual's "persona", his "shadow" and "anima" among these part selves.

Fordham usually defines the self as the original or primal integrate or as the total personality. He sees the various behavioural patterns of which the infant is capable as de-integrations of this original self. Successive de-integrations and re-integrations eventually result in an ego, self-awareness, an identity etc.

There is one paper by Fordham (1974) called "Defences of the self" which deals with schizoid and other archaic defences. This use of the word self to mean something like a myself-feeling or an early ego in Jungian terminology has given rise to some misconceptions because the word self is being used here to mean an early ego or self-representation and not the total personality or the primary integrate. In this paper, the individual is behaving *as if* his whole existence is under threat, and, as in all activities of the shadow, he experiences the bad parts of his personality in projection. It is confusing for a Jungian writer to use the term self in this way without careful explanation.

When I submitted these thoughts to Dr Fordham, he wrote (personal communication) that the self of this particular article was not intended to refer to the self as defined in his other writings or in the general Jungian literature. "As to defences of the self I could not say that these were directly referring to the self. But I do say that the patient behaves *as though* the whole of his existence were threatened." In other words we are dealing with fears which pertain to the schizoid level.

The Present Muddle

I would summarize our present muddle over terms as follows:

(1) The word "self", following Hartmann and Kohut, has for many readers come to mean what the early Freudians, the Kleinians and the Jungians referred to somewhat loosely as the "ego". Or, more strictly, it has come to mean the experience-near, concept-like self-representation that was *part* of Freud's idea of the ego. The word "self" might be avoided and the word "I", "me" or "myself" used as appropriate when we mean "the object of narcissistic libido". While happily adopting Kohut's embracing use of the word "self", many analysts equally happily speak of "ego-boundaries" and "ego-defences", thus combining and confusing pre- and post-Hartmann terminology. Jungians could use the word ego in a loose way to cover the layman's "self" or the "self-concept" of the academic psychologists, but when they write about narcissistic personality disorders they tend to use the word self in the same way as it is defined by Kohut in his earlier writings, which is different from Jung's "self".

(2) The word "self" is, we must admit, perhaps not suitable to describe "total personality, conscious and unconscious" because it is the same word as the lay word which implies personal identity and carries the feeling of "myself". It may sometimes have narcissistic value when used thus. As an exercise in clarity, we should if possible use the precise term to convey the required meaning, whether it be hypothetical primal integrate, or "whole personality", or "non-ego organizing centre" or "numinous part-self symbol" or whatever. The use of the word Self with a capital S

is certainly worth adopting if it is clear we are referring to a greater Self that is superordinate to the ego, or to something like a totality. This usage was suggested but apparently abandoned for the English version of Jung's works. After Kohut, it seems even more necessary.

(3) The primal integrative functions of the psyche, which develop *pari passu* with the sense of self, are sometimes referred to as properties of the ego (mainly by Freudians) or of the self (Jungians).

The functions of integration, defence, repression, of modifying the instincts, containing conflict, postponing gratification etc. sometimes carry "myself" feeling and sometimes do not. Many of the containing, reconciling, transforming functions which are associated with a sound "ego" are introjected from the early experience with the mother mainly by example and by reflection from the mother (see Newton and Redfearn, 1977).

As examples, let us list a few "holding functions". They prevent the patient from schizoid disintegration – going to pieces. They prevent him from feeling utterly abandoned. They ensure his continual subjective existence. They prevent his world becoming meaningless, or a desert or a mechanical nightmare. Now all these holding functions may be performed by the analyst in an analysis which is proceeding well. Furthermore, they can be introjected into the patient's personality when the analyst gradually "fails" to hold in a graded way. We conclude from that fact that the mother can hold the child in this way and that the child introjects these functions from the mother as he becomes more independent and active. These functions are not normally performed consciously by the person's "I" but are part of the taken-for-granted background of living. They go with a sound sense of personal identity and thus could be said to be a relatively unconscious part of the ego or the self. But equally they are not subjectively part of the self at times and belong to the patient's "world". They are functions defined by Hartmann as ego functions, and are usually regarded by Jungians as archetypal properties of the self – the vessel, the temenos etc. Is there some word we can use for these containing and integrative functions? Some of them simply follow from the fact that the patient is in one skin and from various integrative functions of the central nervous system; some of the higher ones are learned, as I have just explained. There is, in fact, a hierarchy of functions of this sort, as Hartmann emphasizes.

In short, Jungians perhaps should not call these primary and acquired integrative, defensive and reality-adapting functions "ego functions", as they are sometimes to do with the "I", sometimes with the "not-I". For the time being they could refer to them as primary or secondary integrative functions of the personality, holding functions, inhibitory functions etc.

Discussion

There is a great deal of agreement among analysts and other psychologists about the development of personal identity and self-awareness, agreement which is masked by the marked differences in terminology. All the authors describe personal identity and the subjective "I" arising out of and resulting from a primal integrative background, but sometimes the personal identity is called the ego and sometimes the self, and sometimes the primary integrate or integrative functions is called the ego and sometimes the self. It is usually easy to discern the usage providing one is aware of the possibility of quite opposing usage of the terms "ego" and "self", particularly in the psychoanalytical literature.

The terminological tools of trade have been laboriously developed by the different schools of analysis, and crude or bad "translation" inevitably does violence to meaning and distorts ways of working. Many years of training are necessary even to enable one to handle one set of tools. Yet this should not prevent our trying to benefit from the experience of other schools, and the foregoing analysis may help in this. The need to help students and trainees orientate themselves in the analytical literature has been the chief spur to me in attempting this correlation.

Whether we call it ego, self-concept or self-representation, the sense of personal identity arises out of some primary, boundaryless yet far from static or uniform sensorium where "I" and "you" are not yet distinct. To the healthy mother, her baby is already a distinct person with a mind of his own, and with several distinct possible "behaviours", not by any means all of which can be carried out at the same time. At the reflex level, and for more and more complex behaviours, complex hierarchies of integrative functions are present from the beginning. As the baby grows up, the various behaviours are further elaborated and modified, and the integrated functions are also elaborated and differentiated. Each of the possible behaviours, as well as the whole baby, tends to actualize itself, to get itself represented in the psyche and to behave as if it were a whole individual defending itself and enhancing itself. The main ego-complex is thus a composite of representations. The archetypes and complexes are called here sub-personalities, each with its own ways of defending itself and relating to other parts of the individual as if each were a person. These ways of relating to each other and evolving are reflected in the mythologies of mankind. Each sub-personality is potentially able to take possession of the feeling of "I", of behaviour, or of both. Much of analysis consists of putting the various sub-personalities in touch with each other, and the ego-complex, the will, the feeling of choice and self-value etc. are of vital importance in providing links in all this integration.

Ideally, the mother recognizes and, with her affect, her behaviour and her talk etc., validates the infant and each of his behaviours or sub-personalities. The various bits of the infant's potential thus become ego-integrated and not ego-alien. Where possible "behaviours" compete, conflict results. The mother at first performs a choosing or holding function. The infant introjects these functions and they become part of the ego-complex (not necessarily conscious, but usually taken for granted unless called into question). Thus it does not seem profitable to me to differentiate ego-functions from "self-representation" as Hartmann and Kohut do. Both develop together. Furthermore, we are so accustomed to talk about ego defences and ego boundaries that we may as well carry on doing so. Narcissism would then have to do with the ego in a broad sense. This is how Jung defined the ego. We should not use the word self in Kohut's sense unless we change to a capital "S" for the Jungian Self to mean the whole personality, or an organizing centre in the unconscious or otherwise something specifically "Jungian". For the everyday meaning of self as having to do with personal identity, and Allport's "proprium", we could continue to use the word self with a lower case "s". We could then talk about the tendency for the Self (primary integrate) to actualize itself, and to represent itSelf in the psyche as the self etc. in a perfectly intelligible way.

Problems similar to those discussed in this chapter are raised – and not dissimilar conclusions are reached – in an article by Rosemary Gordon (1980) about narcissism, the feeling of "I" and the sense of personal identity. She opts for the term "internal object" instead of my term "sub-personality". These internal objects, similar to those of psychoanalytical "object-relations-theory", may, however, be derived from inner, archetypal sources in the personality as well as from outer "objects" (persons, etc.). She points out that the sense of identity is shaped by bodily sensations, memories, images as well as by the mirroring activities of other people, especially the mother. Using case histories, she shows how the feeling of "I" can be taken over first by one internal object, then by another. Her paper relates ego-inflation with possession of the "I" by certain archetypes, but it also attempts to relate these concepts with those of Kohut and other psychoanalysts.

Students of psychology and analytic trainees often need guidance through the confusion of terms used in various schools. The terms "ego" and "self" in analytical literature are, as has been pointed out in this chapter, in some cases used one way and sometimes in the opposite way. For some, the ego emerges from the original self, for some it is the other way round. Yet there is little disagreement about what these terms refer to – personal identity or its precursor arises out of an original un-differentiated or boundaryless integrate or sensorium. The popularity of the writing of Kohut and his followers and the value of their clinical work on narcissistic disorders has now made it particularly urgent to differentiate the self in the everyday sense, and the self which has to do with self-value, from the self as conceived by Jung.

Chapter Two

The Jungian Self

Examples of Self-realization in Jung's Autobiography

Jung's concept of the self and of individuation marked his personal and philosophical maturity, achieved after prolonged self-questioning and self-exploration following the break with Freud. At this point in his life he found what he had sought since childhood, namely, a unified view of science, philosophy and religion, and a way of life for himself. He had found his own way at the same time as clarifying his views of psychic structure. He had found techniques for self-exploration which he named "active imagination".

No dynamic psychology which is not a way of life for its adumbrator deserves to be taken seriously. One's map of the structure of the psyche has to be one's blueprint for living, otherwise it is merely an academic exercise or a confidence trick. The pioneers of psychoanalysis were culture-heroes, shaping out their own professions, their own way of living and of looking at life, and suffering in the process. In this respect we see that Jung was certainly not behindhand, although Freud himself considered Jung retrograde.

In his autobiography *Memories, Dreams, Reflections* (Jung, 1963) Jung devotes little space to his career or his personal life, much to the development of his view of the psyche. He describes how his inner vision, sharpened and nourished from childhood, finally united with his choice of career and his respect for practicalities, in a unified stream which he called the psychological attitude. Out of his personal struggle he achieved his own synthesis.

From an early age he seems to have been unusually able to find meaning and value from his inner life – his dreams, visions and revelations.

One of Jung's grandfathers was an eminent Basel physician of great charm; the other was a distinguished theologian who saw visions

(Ellenberger, 1970, p. 661). Jung's father was a modest country pastor who did not command his son's unqualified respect. Owing to his father's occupation, Jung as a child saw many burials. People of the village sometimes ceased to be around. He was informed that the Lord Jesus had taken them and he knew that they had been committed to holes in the ground. The Lord Jesus evidently devoured people and furthermore was associated in Jung's mind with gloomy men in black coats called Jesuits, whom his father seemed to fear.

One day he had a particularly frightening encounter with one of these Jesuits from which he fled and hid himself in the attic. Now he had his first dream of a divine being, which filled him with fear and awe. In the dream, curiosity led him to explore a hole in the ground. He came to an underground chamber which had a low platform in the centre. On this platform was a magnificent throne, and standing, or sitting, on the throne was a huge erect phallus which reached to the ceiling of the chamber. At the same time he heard his mother's voice saying either "*That* is the man-eater" (i.e. the phallus, not Jesus, is the eater of men) or "That is the *man-eater*" (i.e. Jesus and the man-eating phallus are one and the same). Jung could never decide between the two meanings.

In Jung's own terminology, the royal phallus would be a Self-image or a symbol of the Self. The numinosity, the mystery, the ambiguity, the super-human power and the terror all would be attributes of the divine Self. Yet this regal phallic being clearly cannot be said to represent his whole person or personality; rather, it could be argued that this numinous dream image complemented in an obvious way Jung's child's ego at the time. But experiences such as these permeate the subjective "myself" and may signal a changing relationship between a hitherto unconscious part of oneself (symbolized here by the royal phallus) and the "I". In this instance we are dealing with the child Jung and his greed, his erections and his feelings of power, parts of his personality which at that time were to some degree separated from his experience of himself and his body. We might say that the giant phallus represented a secret, split-off, omnipotent, devouring, phallic part of his personality which could at that time only be experienced as other than himself, as it were in projection (that is, projection into the "not-me"). Other details in dreams such as this in psychotherapy furnish us with clues about the precise nature and progress of the relationship between the part of the personality represented by the dream symbol and the conscious "I". Thus a dream object or person may be coming up, going down deeper, being buried, unearthed, approached, fled from, shrouded in darkness or light, threatening to engulf the dreamer or be engulfed etc.

Jung gives many examples of such "symbols of the self" in his book *Aion*:

> Thus the self can appear in all shapes from the highest to the lowest, inasmuch as these transcend the scope of the ego personality in the manner of a daimon. It goes without saying that the self also has its theriomorphic symbolism. The commonest of these images in modern dreams are, in my experience, the elephant, horse, bull, bear, white and black birds, fishes, and snakes. Occasionally one comes across tortoises, snails, spiders, and beetles. The principal plant symbols are the flower and the tree. Of the inorganic products, the commonest are the mountain and the lake (Jung, 1951, p. 226).

In my own terminology, such symbols would all refer to corresponding sub-personalities. In clinical practice, when we meet one of these "symbols of the Self" in someone we know well, we are often astonished at its appositeness. We often exclaim to ourselves "That's my patient to a T". But of course, to the patient, such an image might well not represent himself or any aspect of himself. Nevertheless, the occurrence of the image usually indicates at least the possibility of an increase in self-awareness.

In the next paragraph Jung says:

> Where there is an undervaluation of sexuality the self is symbolized as a phallus. Undervaluation can consist in an ordinary repression or in overt devaluation (Jung, 1951, p. 226).

No doubt Jung had himself as well as his patients in mind when he wrote this. In his own case, the underground situation suggests the secret aspect of his phallic impulses.

In his autobiography Jung does not even mention the possibility of any relationship between the dream and his own instincts or his own body. Instead he writes of the burying or hiding of his self.

> Now I know that what happened then was a kind of burial in the earth. It was many years before I came out again. It happened in order to bring about the greatest possible amount of light into the darkness. It was an invitation into the realm of darkness. My intellectual life had its unconscious beginnings at that time (Jung, 1963).

He is clearly relating the beginnings of his intellectual development with the exploration of the buried, phallic part of his personality. But, equally clearly, this part of him was not *experienced* by him at the time as part of himself.

From about that time Jung felt himself sorely divided into two distinct sub-personalities, an ordinary everyday schoolboy and a secret possessor of and explorer of forbidden knowledge. This division would seem to parallel a duality he experienced as belonging to his mother, who at times seemed to be a perfectly ordinary mother, and at other times a strange medium or visionary. This duality presumably provided the basis for his ideas about the "introverting" and "extroverting" attitudes of the human psyche.

The hidden yet powerful phallic/Jesuitic part of himself, more powerful than his personal father, seems to have been given concrete symbolic expression in the form of a diminutive carving Jung made of a man with frock coat, top hat and shiny black boots. Jung made a bed for him in his pencil case and placed him with a much treasured oblong black stone from the Rhine. He hid the pencil case in the attic and this helped him to feel safe and less tormented by conflicts. In times of trouble he would steal into the attic and take a look at this secret, powerful "self" which was not subjectively himself but which complemented and strengthened his conscious "myself".

We evidently need a name for these symbols or symbolic objects which, while being related to the self concept or conscious "myself" in a potential or compensatory way, are not representations of the self in the ordinary everyday sense of the word "self", nor yet are they representative of the total personality. They may support, strengthen, comfort or inspire the conscious "myself". They may or may not have a concrete form, yet they are often cherished objects reminding us of Winnicott's "transitional objects", e.g. the cherished piece of material, doll or pet (Winnicott, 1958). It is true that Winnicott defines the transitional object as "the first not-me possession" and derives it from a part of the mother such as the breast, but it is an object which is transitional between "me" and "not me" and can be related to thumb-sucking and one's own body. Although we are dealing with boyhood rather than infancy, the area of play and of transitional phenomena of this sort remains a vital one in the development of the personality.

These symbols or symbolic objects are manifestly related to the "proprium" although not to the "myself". With Jung we could without too much distortion refer to them as "symbols of the self", or we might if we wanted more accuracy refer to them as "transitional self-symbols" or, when appropriate, as symbols referring to "emergent aspects of the self" (i.e. emerging from the unconscious and potentially integrable into the "myself"). Or we might call them symbols of emerging sub-personalities.

We should notice that these Jungian "self-symbols" may take either a gigantic, devouring or a diminutive, cherished form, or both alternately. Depending on circumstances, the "myself" can feel small or large, threatened or protective, in relation to these as yet unrealized parts of the personality. If they loom large, and are assimilated into the "I", we are dealing with an inflation (not necessarily a pathological one of course).

By the age of about eleven, Jung began to experience God as much more real, a Being to whom he could pray without any sense of contradiction in himself. It was very satisfying, he writes, to know that it is impossible to form any correct conception of God. An analogy with the secret in the attic suggested itself to Jung. One day – by then he was twelve – after much agony and fear, he dared to let himself imagine God defaecating on the city's cathedral. We can be sure that Jung was less rather than more consciously using this image of God to express the contempt he (again consciously or unconsciously) felt towards his father and his father's Church. To this extent at least the God image is a Jungian self-symbol. In the questioning and perhaps God-like, contemptuous destruction of some man-made aspects of his religious loyalties, Jung eventually found his own individual approach to religion, separating himself from the values and beliefs of the collective. The vision was in this sense a fore-runner of Jung's concept of individuation. This experience gave him a profound sense of knowledge of and intimacy with God. He felt alone in this true communion, of which he saw no sign in his father or other men of the Church. Nor could he find in Church doctrine any reference to the dark side of God, which to him was a matter of very real and devastating experience.

During his teens, Jung read avidly in philosophy and religion. Meister Eckhart, who for him had the breath of life, and Schopenhauer, who knew of God's dark and blind sides, were the only writers who gave him enlightenment or satisfaction.

If the dream of the phallic divinity, and the vision of the defaecating one, ushered in the secret religious questionings of his teens, two dreams of his late teens seem to have led him to his decision to take up a medical career. The second of these contained one of these emerging sub-personality symbols in a numinous, beautiful form. In the dream Jung was in a wood, and in the darkest place he found a circular pool. Half immersed in the water was the strangest and most wonderful creature, a round animal about three feet across, shimmering in opalescent hues, and consisting of innumerable tiny cells or organs shaped like tentacles. It is easy to see how this image could inspire him to undertake zoological studies. He wanted to study zoology, but his common sense told him he would make a better living in the field of medicine.

Symbols of this sort often act as goals or ideals leading one to achievements and developments in life; thus they lead on to Self-realization. They contain in germinal form (and often in surprising detail when viewed retrospectively) important elements in the future life and activities of the dreamer or recipient of the vision. An ideal city or building, an ideal political or economic organization, an ideal person, an ideal grouping or group of people, may all at times exemplify these symbols. The therapeutic group usually comes to symbolize the Self in the same way for the individuals in it, the various members representing different sub-personalities.

Early in his medical career, Jung studied the visions, ectasies and trances of a girl who was a spiritualistic medium. She had certain hysterical tendencies. Although maintaining scientific scepticism, he takes a positive view of her disorder. From the beginning of his psychiatric interests he took a positive, teleological view of the manifestations of the unconscious even when they are to all appearances maladaptive. The compensatory and the life-enhancing aspects, as well as the dark side, of the unconscious, were very real to him. In this he differed noticeably from the more pessimistic Freud. For example, while both were agreed on the fundamental importance of the incest motif in the unconscious, Jung emphasized the positive, on-going, symbolic aspects of depression, suffering, darkness, and their transformation and use in liberating the personality from the mother and from the regressive need for the mother. Freud, on the other hand, stressed the non-adaptive, wishful, regressive, unattainable aspects of such unconscious fantasies. Whereas Jung regarded the God image as relating to liberation from the actual parents, the attainment of selfhood and the process of individuation, Freud regarded the God image as a wish-fulfilling illusion with which the liberated person must dispense in his quest for self-awareness.

These differences proved irreconcilable at the time and between these two particular men. Perhaps neither realized deeply and personally that one's highest goal and one's deepest regression are but opposite sides of the same coin, a paradoxical truth about the self, both sides of which are difficult to see at the same time. The years 1906–13 saw the blossoming of the collaboration between Freud and Jung and their final break. Jung was thirty-one years old in 1906, and had been working at the Burghölzli Psychiatric Hospital in Zürich for six years. Jung did not have much gratitude or respect either for the hospital or Professor Bleuler, its chief. These difficulties with father figures were predictable and crucial. Jung suffered very greatly after the break with Freud, and within a few months was pursuing in a characteristically courageous way his exploration of his own unconscious.

The next five years were the crucial ones in the development of these explorations and the clarification of his ideas about the self. The method he used differed radically from the free association method used by Freud on his patients and on himself. It consisted of the careful noting of dreams and fantasy material and the conscious stimulation and observation of the fantasies while temporarily suspending a consciously judgmental or actively guiding attitude. It was out of several years of such work at this mid-life watershed of his life (say from the age of 39 to 44) that his theory of the self and his views on individuation emerged. Within weeks, the dreams and fantasies had already attained a terrifying autonomy and intensity, but he managed to avoid a psychotic breakdown by means of his strong commitments to the external world, wife, family, home, patients, and by the careful translation of the findings of his explorations into actions, theoretical formulations, and moral conclusions pertaining to the real world. In all this his experience with psychotic patients and the dangers of introspection must have been crucial.

Through this work Jung's own "sub-personalities" gradually revealed themselves and the archetypes and the theory of archetypes emerged. This story is well told in his autobiography and does not belong here, but certain biases in this self-observation must be noted.

In the first place, there is a grandiose quality, a nobility and a beauty, probably resulting from the second bias, namely, a rejection of any contact that was vulgar, petty or banal as unnecessarily humiliating. He writes:

> When something emotionally vulgar or banal came up, I would say to myself, "It is perfectly true that I have thought and felt this way at some time or other, but I do not have to think and feel that way now" (Jung, 1963).

We could hardly have a clearer statement of the direction of his bias. This flight, as I should call it, from the banal and disgusting is associated by him with a repudiation of the peasants of his childhood

> I had grown up in the country, among peasants . . . incest and perversions were no remarkable novelties to me . . . Along with criminality, they formed part of the black lees that spoiled the taste of life by showing me all too plainly the ugliness and meaninglessness of human existence . . . My whole being was seeking for something still unknown which might confer meaning upon the banality of life (Jung, 1963).

Consistent with this, in some of his dreams and fantasies we have a luminous sub-personality-symbol, for example a scarab or Egyptian dung-beetle, emerging from sewage-like fluids.

Gradually, towards the end of the World War I, as a result of gruelling psychological work on himself, Jung emerged from the darkness, the filth and the gore of his unconscious that had so nearly overwhelmed him. How much "working through" there had been is debatable. One of the principal events marking this emergence was his beginning to understand the mandala drawings which he had for some time found himself creating. During 1918 and 1919, every morning, he sketched a small circular drawing, a mandala, which seemed to him to correspond to his inner situation at that time. Gradually he came to the realization that mandalas are "crypto-grams of the self", which if all is going well, are harmonious, but which do not allow self-deception. In the mandalas he saw his whole being actively at work. Through them and the changes in them, he says, he acquired a living, working conception of the Self. The mandala is a microcosmic representation of the psyche.

As a result of all this work, he began to realize that *the goal of psychic development is the self.* There is no linear evolution, there is merely a circumambulation of the self. All paths lead to the centre, to the mandala, and to individuation. Each circumambulation is a version in miniature of the individuation process. Dream journeys and life quests mean, to me, journeys of the "I" through various areas of the Self, encountering different sub-personalities on the way and developing one's own personal story of progress or lack of it. The goal of the "I" is a subjectively experienced centre like the bull's eye of a target.

In Chapter 9 of this book, I shall be referring to some of the protective and defensive characteristics of these mandalas. I shall be contrasting the *feeling* of wholeness and containment with actually *functioning* as a whole person. Functioning as a whole person is often quite distinct from the *feeling* of wholeness which Jung sometimes associated, perhaps a little naïvely, with the goal of the individuation process.

The often increased *actual* vulnerability of patients in analysis when they achieve a feeling of wholeness and of being safely held was borne in on me shortly before I originally wrote the last paragraph. After much analytical work, a patient of mine achieved some ability to feel held and contained and to feel that she mattered. She painted a pleasant garden landscape with a strong boundary of rocks and an archway or rainbow. On the way home in her motorcar she was enjoying the feeling "Now I can look after myself". While indulging in this pleasant reverie she almost overshot a right turn, braked too violently, and came to a skidding halt halfway up a grass verge and within a foot of the road sign marking the right turn.

A combination of omnipotent *feelings* and of *actual* vulnerability is commonplace in analytical patients. At the time of his mandala drawings it would not be all that surprising to learn, therefore, that Jung was in actuality rather vulnerable and dependent on those around him. He certainly felt isolated and misunderstood, relied a good deal on his family life, and was financially dependent on his wife for his rather grand style of living.

Jung's partial Self-realization, achieved with suffering, is in itself an example of the individuation process. Whereas Freudian analysts may possibly tend to regard the individuation process as occurring only once, when the infant attains autonomy and emerges from symbiosis with the mother, Jungians tend to see essentially the same process occurring all the time, in different ways and at more and more mature levels. The separating out from collective values and the self-awareness which Jung achieved in maturity would be a not untypical example of the individuation process as it is met in adulthood. Thus for the Jungian, the first, mighty steps of the infant towards selfhood are but the beginning of the way of individuation.

Deeply upset and isolated, Jung sought to understand the theoretical differences between himself and Freud in terms of differences in basic personality type. He interpreted the difference in terms of a perennial opposition within the human psyche between extroversion and introversion. He dealt with these two opposing attitudes in a very thoroughgoing way in his book *Psychological Types* (Jung, 1920). The optimum of life as Jung saw it at that time was something like a Middle Way, not of compromise but of a higher synthesis. In the West the Mediator is, or has been, the Messiah, the childishness of which conception, he thought, was self-evident. The East, on the other hand, has for centuries always had an essentially *psychological* doctrine of salvation which brings deliverance within the compass of human intention. The redeeming path is a conscious attempt to find release from the conflict of these and other opposites. For example, Brahma combines the concepts of Creator, divine essence, he in whom all opposites are reconciled, the state of detachment from emotional fluctuations and oppositions, and Self. Jung treats the concept of Tao, the celestial path of reconciliation between the all pervading opposites of Yin and Yang, in a similar way, identifying it with the Self.

Jung's important concept of the symbol, developed at the same time, treats the living symbol, as distinct from the mere token or sign, as the expression of the middle path, the higher synthesis, the living expression of the inexpressible. The symbol is a creative product of the unconscious on the one hand, and of an ego capable of seeing beyond mere actuality on the other. It combines rational and irrational, inner and outer reality. It is Nature's way of containing otherwise unbearable tensions. At this time, for Jung, these "symbols of the Self" could be regarded as the highest or ultimate transcendent functions (symbols).

By 1928, in his essay "The relations between the ego and the unconscious (Jung, 1928), Jung had clearly worked out his conception of a normal working relationship between the "I" and "not-I" parts of the Self, and of pathological forms of I/not-I relationship such as depression, inflation and persona-identification. In his model of the psyche at that time there is an external world which includes other people, and an internal world which includes the personal unconscious and the archetypes of the collective unconscious. The ego relates to both inner and outer worlds and is buffeted by one and the other as between hammer and anvil. The persona is the complex whereby the ego relates to the outer world, but it tends to be collective in its essential nature. Individuation is the process whereby one differentiates oneself from the persona on the one hand and from the collective images on the other. The aim of analysis is the assimilation of the collective psyche.

In a successful analysis, Jung said, first the contents of the personal unconscious are analysed, but then more and more fantasies from the non-personal unconscious emerge and are gradually seen to pursue definite lines of direction which converge on a definite goal, the goal of the individuation process. The assimilation of these unconscious contents carries the twin dangers of inflation and of being overwhelmed by depression. Analysis of the persona is often accompanied by feelings of god-likeness and disorders of the body image such as sensations of levitation, flying, gigantism, dwarfism and other effects similar to those of hallucinogenic drugs. There is a danger of physical illness at this time. "There is a temptation at this time", Jung says "to plunge into the ocean of divinity and, losing all memory, to merge with it." This temptation is the same as the longing for the archetypal mother, from whom we came and to whom we long to return. Resistance of this temptation may lead on to the attainment of the treasure in a form we can use. The true end of analysis, then, is adequate knowledge of the methods of making and maintaining fruitful contact with the unconscious parts of the Self.

Jung's later years were spent in the exploration of the archetypal motifs and in particular the sequences of the images and themes representing the individuation process (*Coll. Wks* **9–14**). The remarkable and detailed correspondences between the symbols of his individuation process, of the versions of it as seen in his patients, and the texts of the alchemists, the gnostics, and the myths of the world, all helped to validate his findings and reduce his feeling of isolation.

Jung's two great theoretical formulations, of the archetypes of the collective unconscious and of the four functions of thinking, feeling, sensation and intuition, both arose out of his self-exploration during the years of World War I. The sub-personalities which emerged included a hero figure, a little brown turd man whom he regarded as his shadow, an old man calling himself Elijah, a beautiful blind girl calling herself Salome and a black snake. He concluded that all these products of imagination represented important parts or functions of his own personality. In his 1925 seminars he related how these figures were the origin of his ideas about the four functions. At first he identified the Salome or anima figure with the function of feeling, Elijah with thinking, but he later separated out his theory of archetypes from that of the four functions.

In the same seminars Jung spoke of an experience which was important in contributing to his concept of the Self. He was pursuing his imaginative conversations and transactions with the figures I have just mentioned. The serpent wrapped itself around him and a struggle ensued, whereupon Jung found himself transformed into the lion-headed god Aion, uniting animal and divine attributes and reconciling male and female aspects so that, like the god, he contained all within himself.

Another type of experience contributing to his concept of the Self arose out of his mediumistic powers. During 1916 he was compelled from within to make further acquaintance with the "thinker" figure. He experienced first profound restlessness, then an ominous atmosphere of ghostly presences around him. Other members of his family noticed the atmosphere: the doorbell was rung by an unseen hand. The place was filled with spirits of the dead who cried "We have come back from Jerusalem where we found not what we sought". These were the first words of his "Seven sermons to the dead", which he wrote down as if the words were simply flowing out of him over the course of the next three evenings. The ghostly manifestations ceased as he began to write. For him, the dead became ever more clearly "the voices of the Unanswered, Unresolved, and Unredeemed . . . These conversations with the dead formed a kind of prelude to what I had to communicate to the world about the unconscious" (Jung, 1963, pp. 183–4). It was then, Jung says, that he ceased to belong merely to himself, or to have the right to do so.

I mention this incident to show that, although Jung does not go beyond his own experience, his notion of the collective unconscious transcends matter, the material body, personal experience and ordinary physical time.

It was soon after "The seven sermons" that Jung started to draw mandalas daily. He does not say how they differed from each other, but he mentions that one day he received a disturbing letter from a Salome-like woman. The mandala on that day looked as if it had burst. The climax of his mandala activity Jung regarded as the culmination of his personal development. At this time he had a dream in which the mandala took the form of a city, Liverpool, the Pool of Life, bathed in darkness and rain. In a raised area in the middle of the city, he and his companions found a broad square. The various quarters of the city were formed by streets converging on the square. In the centre of the square was a round pool, and in the centre of this an island. The island was ablaze with sunlight, and on it was a magnolia tree, a shower of reddish blossoms. The tree stood in the light and was at once the source of the light. Jung's companions did not see the tree, and talked with surprise of another Swiss living in one of the secondary, dark streets. This referred to his real life as he saw it at the time; unpleasant, off-centre, dark and sustained only by the inner vision.

If we look at the mandala which Jung painted of this dream (Jung, 1950a, Concerning Mandala Symbolism, Fig. 6), we see that there is a central square which is open to the outside of the city via radially arranged streets. There is an octagon immediately inside this square which is connected to the square by four "streets"; inside this is a series of circles and a central luminous flower-like arrangement. This inner region of circles and "flower" is cut off, or protected, from the "outside world". But these inner rings communicate with each other via radial channels. So we have an outer system based on the square and straight lines which is dark and in communication with the outer world, and an inner system based on circles, curves and light which has no obvious connection with the outer system. This inner system Jung regarded as representing the true centre of his personality and as his inner vision. His finding of a true centre of his personality which did not correspond with his conscious "I" or "myself" was for Jung the vital discovery concerning the individuation process.

The disconnection between the outer and inner systems shows us how things were for Jung when he painted this mandala. But we do not know the exact reasons for this defensive disconnection, which in clinical practice may vary from one day to the next. In analysis it is sometimes possible to understand details such as this and see them change as defences are resolved or modified.

We shall leave Jung at this point in his personal development. Jung's autobiographical material has simply been used to show that whether he uses the concept of the self to refer to

(1) the total personality, or
(2) conscious ego plus personal and collective unconscious, or
(3) the image of God, or
(4) compensatory, emergent symbols arising out of the unconscious and leading to an expansion of interests or of awareness,

there is a common element in his usage of the word Self. There is always a sense of something super-ordinate to the conscious "I" with great potency and with organizing characteristics. "Symbols of the Self" in this Jungian sense can lead us to the discovery of hitherto unexplored regions of ourselves, for example the phallic divinity of Jung's memoirs, or they may lead us to our "true path", our "true selves", our destiny (for example, the "jelly fish" symbol "leading" Jung into biology). They are consciousness-expanding, whether they lead us outwards, or inwards, forwards or backwards in time (or preferably, all four at once, of course).

A Discussion of Jung's Concept of the Self

In the foregoing sketch of Jung's development I have drawn attention to the following characteristics:

(1) His secret phallic power.
(2) His feeling of nearness to God and his contempt for his personal father.
(3) His sense of inner vision and destiny, combined with his feelings of being threatened by outside forces.

(4) His apparent avoidance of some bodily aspects of oneself, e.g. the anal aspects, together with his avoidance of the ignoble, even of the banal.
(5) His enormous achievement in synthesizing his religious, philosophical and medical psychological lines of enquiry. God is not "out there", nor a mere self-projection. In his own experience, the archetypes, including the Self considered as archetype, have some extra-material reality. (He did not attempt to work out the connection between the archetypal and the physical world but attempted to bridge the split with his concept of synchronicity.)

The limits or boundaries of the Jungian Self are impossible to define. They extend far beyond Allport's "proprium", which in turn extend far beyond the material body. There is of course a very real sense in which we are all part of each other and all part of past and future history, and we do not know the relationship between our material selves and ourSelves in this wider sense. There is of course a close relationship between the "I" feeling, the self-image, the body-world schema, and the body image, probably at a neurophysiological level, but this is quite a different matter from crudely equating our material bodies with our selves.

The clinical value of Jung's concept of the Self is perhaps not appreciated by non-Jungian analysts and others. It stresses the forward-pointing, not merely wishful or compensatory, functions of the unconscious parts of the psyche and gives full value to the actual symptoms, the symbols, and the behaviour of the analysand and instead of reducing him and his status in relation to the analyst. Let me give an over-simplified clinical example.

Suppose that a child patient dreams at Christmas time of a greedy, staring wolf outside his bedroom window. If we are in the habit of regarding animal and other dream symbols as sub-personality symbols, we should in the first instance tend to think of the wolf as representing the child's greedy feelings, split off from his "myself" but nevertheless stimulated by Christmas time in an understandable way. We should tend to postulate that here we have a child who is unable to contain his greedy devouring feelings in his "myself", so that it is projected on to the wolf outside the window, no doubt via the parental images. If we do not think of the wolf *in the first instance* as a sub-personality image but as a parental image, we might simply follow the path of free association, as Freud did in a case like this (Freud, 1914). This might or might not lead us eventually to experiences in the oral stage of development which resulted in the alienation of the oral cravings.

Freud in fact demonstrates, or at least provides evidence for, a fuller interpretation of the wolf image in this dream. In addition to greedy

Christmas-time feelings, we have scopophilic greed regarding a primal scene experience in which the patient identifies with the father, and we are dealing with homosexual, masochistic and cannibalistic wishes. Thus Freud's further findings amplify and modify, but do not contradict, our tentative interpretation which would tend as an initial hypothesis to look on the wolf as a split-off sub-personality or self-symbol.

However, in following these paths of association, the living, dynamic qualities of the symbol and the chance of ego-enhancement in acceptance of the wolf-in-oneself may be obscured or for the time being lost. It might not result in the establishment of a living, useful connection between the patient and his greedy feelings, or in a useful coming-to-life of the alienated part of the self, in the first place as a "living symbol". The relationship of the "wolf-in-the-patient" to his "I" is of prime interest in a Jungian analysis. It may be in other psychotherapies also, but of that I am not at all certain. Keeping this relationship in the forefront of one's mind can lead to illuminating clinical observations of the appearances and behaviours of the patient which would otherwise simply not be made.

A few days before I originally wrote this, one of my patients dreamt of someone about to strangle him from behind. Discussing the dream, he spoke of his life being strangled by money worries, uncongenial work, a restrictive society, and by the attitude of me the analyst and of previous analysts. While he was working up to these assertions, I noticed that he was using his hands in the manner of a strangler, and suggested that the strangler image might also be in part a self-image. This enabled us to link the neck with the penis, strangulation with masturbation and with his hatred of his mother. To have dealt with the strangler only "in projection" on to his environment would have been a far less thoroughgoing way of working.

The need to reject parts of one's total personality as parts of the subjective "I", and on the contrary to project them on to the outside world or on to others, is of course all part of character-formation. One's character determines what one regards as part of the "I" and what one regards as "not-I". The needs of bodily health and personal survival in infancy ensure the existence of these essentially paranoid or narcissistic defences in us. The personal identity develops out of the totality of possibilities of the personality, depending on parental and other social pressures. Jung taught that if the "I" develops in a biased or distorted way, and is not in tune with the Jungian Self, the unconscious servo-mechanisms of the total personality will always be working to redress the balance. Hence the usually compensatory relationship between dreams, symptoms, unconscious behaviours and other manifestations of the unconscious, on the one hand, and the conscious attitude on the other.

Jung regarded this differentiation of the conscious "I" out of the unconscious as a continuing process, far from a once-for-all affair. The infant needs to be held, supported and also limited by the mother, and he also needs to achieve autonomy and freedom. These opposite needs sometimes alternate, sometimes co-exist, and sometimes oppose each other. In this continuing drama the images of the hero, the witch, the devouring dragon and the Cross of self-sacrifice (crucifixion) may become constellated and may acquire meaningfulness. The hero myth is the largely unconscious intra-psychic drama in projection. The hero often has more than human stature: he has godlike qualities. Since, says Jung, he is an archetype of the Self, his divinity only confirms the numinosity of the Self or its share in the divine (Jung, 1912). "It is a psychological fact", he says "that the Self is an image of the divine and *cannot be distinguished from it empirically*." The hero corresponds with the "mana" personality. Identification with him (confusing feeling hero-like with being a hero) may lead to the disaster of inflation, and this helps us put the numinosity of the hero in perspective. The contrast and interplay between the omnipotent and divine self, to be enjoyed or to be sacrificed for love, and the everyday self of ordinary reality, is a major theme of this book and is dealt with at some length in Chapter 4. Jung's emphasis is primarily on the divine aspects and is essentially therapeutic and optimistic.

We can talk of the differentiation of the "I" and of personal identity out of the total repertoire of the personality. We can also talk of the development in childhood of a stable self-representation or of a realistic self-image rooted in body feeling and containable bodily attitudes and impulses. How much anger, how much sexual feeling and emotion, how much excitement of all kinds we can hold and use in and with our bodily selves and be responsible for will depend on our inherent qualities and on the quality of mothering we had, among other things. This will determine how much of our potential is alienated or sacrificed, and acted out unconsciously or experienced in projection. It is not determined once for all: changes are occurring throughout life. Individuation, or portions of the individuation sequence, are occurring throughout life, more at some critical times than others.

While acknowledging that separation of "I" and "not-I", the achievement of the feeling that one is an individual person and the beginning of play have instinctive foundations and are not even confined to human beings, we must not lose sight of the important element of self-awareness and self-involvement in Jung's concept of individuation. Personal struggle, personal conflict and the clash of conflicting wishes are of course experienced by the child, but not in the same way as by the adult with his more differentiated sense of personal identity, loyalties and moral attitudes. We slide at various times between the almost unconscious acting-out of habitual or instinctive functioning and spiritual revelation and agonizing conflict. Few of us equal Jung in the heights and depths of awareness, the amounts of energy involved, in his individuation problems.

Experiences of revelation and of conversion, as well as of the numinous aspects of the self, share some of the characteristics of epileptic, irradiating excitation of the nervous system. One should include primal experiences and the "primal scream" phenomena in this category. They all involve a breakthrough of the "not-I" part of the personality into the "I" part, the "conscious ego". This flooding or irradiation crosses normal barriers and may suffuse the entire "I" including the body image (see Chapters 3 and 6). Here we are dealing with the "mystical marriage" of conscious and unconscious (see Jung, 1955/1956).

If, by way of recapitulation, we attempt an inventory of the contents of the Jungian Self, we start off with the self of everyday usage, with its feelings of continuity, integrity, stability (or not, of course). In a wider sense there is one's personal identity.

Then we have the "sub-personalities" resulting from introjection. Suppose "I" am timid because I had a crushing father. I usually behave timidly towards others, on to whom I tend to project the crushing father. But towards my children, say, or when I am tired etc., I behave like a crushing father. So the timid child and the crushing father are interlinked sub-personalities (to do with my crushing-father-complex), parts of the Jungian Self.

These sub-personalities would all be based in the first instance on Jungian archetypes or archetypal interactions, and so we have the archetypes and archetypal images, including the God image or images, as components of the Jungian Self. In clinical work, it is necessary to appreciate the split-off, infantile omnipotence projected as the God image, and to help the patient recover this and other parts of the Self lost or sacrificed in the development of the patient's self or character. The notion of archetypes complements the notion of the organism reacting to external circumstances, things and people. Both notions are useful.

A more mature "I" will be able to contain, rather than act out, intrapsychic conflict. He will experience conflicts and contradictions within himself rather than "going to war" against an enemy representing an alien part of himself. Symbols in the Jungian sense often take the form of symbols reconciling opposite elements, or convey the immense energy involved in these conflicts.

One's wholeness, says Jung, implies a tremendous tension of opposites paradoxically at one, as in the Cross, their most perfect symbol (Jung, 1912, p. 303).

The image of opposing elements meeting, with the liberation or absorption of immense quantities of energy, good or bad, is so all-pervasive that it is hardly possible to exaggerate its psychological importance. This is the energy underlying, for example, primal scene excitement at its most archaic level, schizoid splitting and schizoid defences, the illuminating, shattering properties of the God image, and this is the energy underlying the individuation process. One symbol, that of the Cross, "contains" the most cruel, sadistic torture, given and received, and sublime self-sacrifice and redemption. Jung's notion of the self therefore goes to the heart of the question of the ultimate nature and source of psychic energy, the harnessing or the destructive effects of this energy, and the inspiring properties of symbols.

These symbols are often idealized rather than fully assimilated. When they are worked through and more fully realized, life becomes richer, sounder, fuller, yet often in a sense more "ordinary". I am thinking of several of my own patients in whom such symbols of opposites clashing or meeting were almost unbearable in their energy. In all these patients we had to work through a great mass of split-off, sado-masochistic material and behaviour before the energy could be incorporated into the "I", the personal body-based I. Responsibility could then be taken for these parts of the personality and acting out could cease. The very brilliance and energy of these numinous symbols may be a measure of how much work still needs to be done in their integration.

Some of these numinous symbols have a cosmic quality. This may mean that affects pertaining to ordinary relationships are being denied. To a person in a symbiotic relationship, a difference of opinion with the symbiotic partner may be followed by a dream of cosmic catastrophe. Analysis may help such a person achieve a measure of separation and individuation by helping him face the psychic reality of the catastrophe. He has to dare risk the expected catastrophe, and when it does not happen in quite the feared way, he may dare more. As real life differences are faced and resolved, the cosmic dream catastrophes and images tend to assume more human proportions. The "I" includes more, the "not-I" is less idealized, less terrifying and more separate.

Chapter Three

God and myself, God as myself

The subject matter of this chapter will be the quite ordinary religious experiences of myself and one or two of my patients. I shall not, I hope, be too dogmatic about the nature of God, but I shall take it for granted that experiences of a meaningful kind that could (albeit rather vaguely) be called religious are commonplace.

I do not claim to have any personal relationship with anything like a God-person. I do not dismiss such experiences as illusory, but I am not the sort of person to have them. I have a none-too-confident view that psyche and energy/matter are inter-related, and that underlying these, and more basic than time, there is some infinitely differentiating unity. We might call this God but this is perhaps not important. What matters most in my view is religious experience, the sort of experience that only needs to happen once for a person's entire life or outlook on life to be transformed.

More than thirty years ago, when I had such an experience, I would have liked to "shout it from the rooftops". Now I am only using it because it is the only such experience that I can describe from the inside, and because only personal experience in this field is likely to be of any interest to the reader. The autobiographical notes in this chapter will, I hope, provide some background for the later chapters in this book, in a similar way to the way I used Jung's autobiography to make more meaningful the peculiarities of his concept of the self.

Childhood Experiences

When I was two or three years old, before I had been indoctrinated by adults, I think I took some sort of re-incarnation for granted. Not that I knew very much about death anyway, as far as I recall. I had a very hazy division between wishes, dreams and "reality". Yet I believe I may well have had a more direct experience of fundamental reality than I do now.

For my first three years I was an only child, close to my mother. When she was angry she flashed green lightning from her eyes and looked like a witch – a word and figure I learned about much later. What I actually "saw" antedated external knowledge. When she was holding me and talking to me, she was a divine golden Person, a paradise landscape. When I was three, my second brother was born, and disillusion entered my life. A polarity between "dream" and "reality" was established. I became morose, sulky, self-sufficient and stoical. Yet there was an enhanced intellectual bond between my mother and myself. She taught me to read before I went to school at four years of age, and I remember spending happy times with her at blackboard and slate, drawing houses and trains and making the letters of the alphabet.

I had a toy engine at this time, a wooden imitation of a steam locomotive big enough to sit and ride on, and I used to push myself along with a kind of running action. One day its funnel came off and was lost. That night I dreamt that God, or my father (they were not clearly distinguished from each other) had put the funnel back. Next morning I rushed downstairs expecting a miracle, but I do not think I was very surprised that this was not the case. I think this was the first time I made a conscious distinction between dream and "reality". Of course my disillusionment had its compensations – I now was no longer so afraid of my frightening dreams and could now dismiss them as "only dreams". A few years later fact, truth and science were what I put my faith in, while feelings, daydreams, imagination and religion were relegated to lower status and even avoided when possible. My preference for facts and "reality" was due to a fear of the irrational – its ghosts, witches, phantoms and night fears.

In this story of an early disillusionment, I am making a connection between my assumption of some kind of immortality, the absence of boundaries between dream and reality, and an essentially unbroken and taken-for-granted security in or with my mother, which somehow included my father. In the ensuing period of loss or separation I turned towards my father, towards a fatherly God, who might restore my lost "phallic omnipotence" as symbolized by the lost engine funnel and the belief in its magical restoration. Later, the basic unity of my mother-world was replaced by a duality in which the mother elements were consciously abrogated and the thinking, masculine elements of science and realism are consciously espoused (see also my article on things and persons; Redfearn, 1982).

It seems arguable that had I known that I or my father could and would find and repair the funnel, then I would not have had the wish-fulfilling dream (nor the subsequent disillusionment). My dream father-God would not have been needed. It is not easy to demonstrate in this instance that the helpful dream-father-God was of any use. But one could cite many instances where such a figure apparently supplies vital help and support when needed. More important to the present argument is the part played by the God-image in the separation from the mother, from the basic unity of the "myself" with the mother/universe.

The God Image Provides a Link with the Lost Mother

A similar function was apparently served by the God image (experience) of one of my analysands. He was born during World War II and was brought up by his mother almost without male help for four or five years. When his father returned from the war he seemed very stern and primitive. The child, however, was often helped by a voice which he identified as the voice of God, exhorting him to "hang on and not lose heart" (the sort of language used by my analysand himself as a result of his English private education). The memory of this voice was always treasured by my patient. God was a super-father or grandfather, who helped him to maintain integrity and pride and to avoid the twin dangers of rebellion on the one hand and abject surrender to the tyrant on the other. On the less positive side, perhaps, my patient's attitude to his real father remained markedly ambivalent, and subsequent authority figures in his life were idealized and feared by turns. In other words, there was not an adequate "working-through" of this ambiguous father image in a personal relationship such that the father figure could become more of a good-and-bad, human, being. The real father failed to establish a sufficiently good relationship with him, the parents' marriage failed and the son came to me because of career and marriage problems of his own.

Again, in this case too, the boy's experience of God could well be of a compensatory character, filling in the vacuum left by the absence for so long of a real, human father. According to this view, Nature causes us to seek and find experiences we lack and even *feel* the lack of. The experience of God was clearly of this kind. This vacuum-filling aspect of Nature might of course be a property of the Divine.

Now in my experience of God and that of my analysand, God the Father is "out there" helping me, encouraging me, letting me hope. He may be part of my (Jungian) Self, experienced in projection, but he is not *experienced* as part of myself because I on the contrary am feeling impotent and in need of help. "Out there" is the natural way of experiencing a powerful, helpful great person, real or illusory, when one is feeling small and helpless.

To continue my own story, my "faith" as a practical working faith was constantly modified by experience and sustained by my family during latency and adolescence. No doubt it was later the basis of my practical working faith in the unconscious. An experience which made a deep impression on me occurred in my very early teens when one evening I was struggling with my mathematics homework. One problem proved insoluble, and the more I tried, the more thick-headed I became. My mother advised me to go to bed and sleep, and prophesied that I should have the solution when I awoke in the morning. And so it proved.

In my own case I have no doubt that the close relationship with my mother in my first three years of life was continued, after the birth of my brother, in a faith that things would "turn out alright" – modified by later experience. It caused me to turn to God and my father when my brother was born, and it enabled my patient to turn to God to combat his real father. But the compensating function of the unconscious is not entirely determined by the past. It is a property of some fundamental organizing and formative principle that we call the primary integrative functions and which we associate with the Jungian Self. Something outside the "myself", outside consciousness, but nevertheless clearly something to do with me in a broad sense. This Self is not only more than the "myself" I know; it is more than the self that other people can see or experience in me. If one understood "God" to mean the totality of one's being, or the totality of all being, one would be clearly speaking of the Self as I have just described it. However, this would be a somewhat introverted view of God and arguably too limited a view of the Deity. But it is also self-evident that God-like feelings and ideas of the infinite, harmonious and all-creative are only a small part of oneself.

The next incident that I wish to use to illustrate a further step occurred when I was six years old. My mother had always taught me that fighting and even anger and depression were unworthy. She herself tried with considerable success to be cheerful, humble, unselfish and unaggressive. But she had flashes of powerful anger when crossed, and like her, I could not be pushed too far without showing fight. I was on one occasion engaged in a fist fight with an overbearing elder cousin when my mother entered the room. To my surprise, instead of quelling the uproar, she was swept away by partisan sentiments and started shouting encouragements to me. I found this very amusing, but a little embarrassing because of the inconsistency between her professed beliefs and her behaviour. I am ashamed to say that I felt morally a little superior to her in some way, more able to tolerate the tension between conflicting feelings, perhaps, than she was. From that moment I became more outside her, more free of an uncritical participation in her feelings, more aware of her contradictions. I am not claiming any actual moral superiority to her, but merely describing a feeling.

These are not endearing qualities in a boy. The ensuing years saw a continuation of the same smug trend. I became absorbed in scientific interests but also enjoyed the atmosphere and the music of church services. I sometimes prayed to a fatherly God who lived mainly in the blue ceiling of our local church and who looked like a composite of my bearded grandfather and the bearded King George V. I now realize as I write this that, at the age of sixty-four, I look extremely like that childhood image of God except that I wear spectacles. I was not sure He really existed but the more anxious I felt the more comfort He was, like the idea of home and the major chord that hymns and other music always ended on in those days.

I very much enjoyed singing in the choir in my early teens, I adored the anthems, I sometimes prayed to a God I came to regard as a scientific nonsense and I dismissed the Bible as scientifically untrue. Truth was mainly what mattered – factual, scientific truth was the highest value of all. When I was thirteen our bishop talked to us at a children's service, and asked us what God was like. I answered that he was like a human being. He agreed and asked why we knew this. I replied that in the book of Genesis it was written that God created man in his own image. He seemed satisfied with this answer, and I wondered whether the bishop was foolish enough not to entertain the possibility that Man had "created" God in his own image. I felt ashamed of myself for giving the acceptable answer rather than my true opinion, and at the same time I felt cynical, sad and lonely.

A Search for a Way

I was by now thoroughly aware of a search for something in life, I knew not what. I sometimes visualized this something as a green jewel. At the university, science and religion seemed more polarized than ever. At one point I made a deliberate attempt to abandon reason as the less important consideration and to plunge into the Christian faith. I joined a student Christian group and during one summer vacation joined a mission to the hop-pickers in Kent. As the only medical student I was in charge of the medical hut, where I saw in the children the permanent and ghastly results of poverty and ignorance. Whereas the other "missionaries" cared more about the souls of the poor, I felt that their ignorance, illness and poverty were more pressing and important claims on me. With some relief to be thinking with much more of my whole mind again, I veered towards socialism and a materialist-historical outlook, reinforced by my studies in the Cambridge type of psychology under Sir Frederick Bartlett, a benign and scholarly man who could talk for an hour and a half on some subject such as the Wurzburg School of Imageless Thought and leave one feeling refreshed and enlightened by his smiling presence, though not greatly interested in the actual content of his meticulous argument.

One had to learn to discuss the "behaviourist" as opposed to the "introspectionist" approach to psychology. We equated "subjective" with prejudice and wishful thinking and with lack of scientific validity. But it seemed to me like arguing which side of a penny is more important, heads or tails. I wrote essays arguing that consciousness was new learning, new conditioning (as opposed to habits and established conditioned reflexes). I had little difficulty reconciling behaviourism and introspection, science and religion, my religious mother and my materialistic, sensible aunt (who was a second mother to me) in terms of my two-sides-of-a-coin image.

But all this had little to do with people or politics. Although I joined a leftist group of students when studying at Johns Hopkins University I found the behind-the-scenes machinations distasteful and felt that the means we used did not justify the extremely unimpressive ends. I withdrew from this group and continued my own search. I still pictured my quest as a search for a green jewel somewhere: even now I do not have much idea why what I sought was often imagined in that particular way.

The polarity between subjective and objective truth seemed at that time to have endless and painful ramifications. Is a statue just so much stone, is a corpse just so much matter, and what is a flag, a National Anthem, a Christ worshipped only by a minority, where is the truth and the ultimate validity of such symbolic objects and customs? Even to brush one's hair or to eat properly seemed like a conformist betrayal of fundamentals, yet we at Cambridge happily wore mortar boards and academic gowns because (we told ourselves) we were made to do so by the entrenched powers of the university, and the fact that "gown" liked to differentiate itself from "town" had to be denied.

Towards the end of my medical studies in Baltimore I came across a series of books by Sorokim which not only discussed these and other polarizations of thought and attitude, but showed how these polarizations permeated philosophy, art, science, the law and politics, not only in the present day but throughout the history of Western culture. His books, and Jung's comparable masterpiece, *Psychological Types* (Jung, 1920) which I read a year or two later, were books after my own heart, books of sufficient breadth, vision and tolerance to free the spirit and gladden the heart. I read voraciously and ruminated endlessly, and might well have become psychotic for a time if I had not had to pass my medical examinations and get a job. Having done this, I soon found myself in psychiatry, involved in the "fantasies" and "delusions" of my patients, with my own ideas about reality again in the melting pot, with no parental figure, no wise man, who seemed capable of helping.

A Religious Experience?

I was in the middle of my first year at the Maudsley Hospital in London. The atmosphere there was scientific rather than religious, if one tries to use that dimension. Some such polarization at that time expressed itself as "Is mental disease due to electrical and chemical malfunction of the brain or is it due to psychological causes?" To be on the wrong side at the Maudsley Hospital was then a danger to one's career. I have since analysed Maudsley doctors who dared not let it be known that they were in analysis, while yet benefiting greatly from it. It was known then as a rather cold and inhuman place, although I personally have the warmest memories of it, and of the friends I had there.

I was reading Aldous Huxley's book *The Perennial Philosophy* (Huxley, 1946) at the time. He seemed to take a broad, almost non-religious, view of God while giving full value to religious experience and prayer. I found the book a great comfort to me at that time, a time at the beginning of one's psychiatric career, when every patient's symptoms, experiences, both neurotic and psychotic, are or have been one's own to some degree, and the boundary between the illusory and the real assumes persecutory intensity. The book gave comfort, and moreover without too great an affront to reason or intellect.

Perhaps I did have a psychosis. I soon found that by adopting a passive yet open and attentive state, suggested by my reading of the book, at first for a few minutes on retiring to bed, then later at odd moments during the day when duties permitted, I was able to allow myself to have an experience which I would call religious. Simply by not resisting, I allowed a God to enter me and my life that was not a God, or any thing or person in particular, but simply some sort of flowing in of energy from the "not-me" into the "myself". It was, I think, the experience that people often describe as God entering one's mind and body; an enlightenment filled my mind and brought my body to fresh life and health. The experience was ecstatic at times, similar to the experiences one may have while falling in love, or that which mystics may have.

The "I" was being inflated by powerful sub-personalities of the "not-I". It was felt, sensorially even, as an almost audible inflowing of God. There was certainly a degree of inflation and denial, in that unrealistically unselfish solutions to my personal problems suggested themselves, and later these solutions needed to be modified so as to reconcile themselves with practical reality. In a state of universal benevolence there was less sharpness than normally in my feelings about particular people, including those closest to myself. For weeks I was in a state of peace and happiness. I knew exactly how psychotic patients feel when they assert that they are Jesus Christ – only I verbalized it to myself in a more sophisticated and actually, one must admit, a less psychotic way. I would have said

I had Christ-like feelings. Long-forgotten passages of the Bible came back to me like joyous illuminations and I felt a new understanding of them. Also, sayings of my grandmother and of my parents came back to me from my childhood.

During the period of "letting in God", the experience was very largely under my conscious control as far as its intensity was concerned. The inflow was accompanied by a rushing sensation in my ears which I was also able to turn on or off, up or down. I wondered whether the rushing sensation was due to hyperactivity of the muscle which tenses the eardrum, in keeping with the general feeling of alertness and expectation. I was reminded of the Holy Ghost entering people with a rushing of wind. Another physiological curiosity: I noted that I could "see" my alpha rhythm much more clearly in the semi-darkness than I could normally. And I think that it was slower in frequency than my "normal" alpha rhythm.

In this state of inflow of "God", the problem – of whether "God" exists as an external reality or whether He is merely a projection of omnipotent feelings – no longer existed. Indeed this utterly satisfying experience of God, oneself and the world as One was the insight which seems to have left the strongest impression on me since that time; of all the aspects of that never-to-be-forgotten experience, it has remained with me as the perfectly satisfying answer to the major "philosophical" problems which had beset me until that time. I would not like to say that this experience was an intimation of the Self in Jung's sense, but it obviously had features in common with Jung's experiences. It felt to me that I had answered the bishop's question, to my own satisfaction at least.

It is a sad commentary on our times in some ways, that I thought it prudent to keep the experience to myself, though I felt like proclaiming it to the world, like a person bursting with love does.

I am unable to give full details of my personal relationships at the time, but it must be said that before the experience there was intense anxiety, fear of a nervous breakdown of some sort and a failure to obtain help or comfort from any actual person, including parental figures. During the experience there was further separation from my actual parents, and no doubt, a kind of regression to a more archaic state of union or fusion with a loved "Other". I was reminded of Christ's saying "Who are my father and my mother?"

Such an experience of the divine is not uncommon, in my work with patients, following separation from loved persons. Sometimes it can be regarded as a manic denial of dependence, on the analyst for instance. It is not always wise to dismiss these experiences in these terms, concentrating on what is being "denied" rather than what is being positively experienced. An experience which is remembered all one's life, and as one of the most valuable in one's life, obviously should not be dismissed in this way. As I have said, the person having such an experience may often appear pathetically vulnerable and out of contact to the outside observer. Perhaps that was so with me – one of my friends said that I seemed to be "in the doldrums" during that period, though for all practical purposes I was working normally (I think). Subjectively my mind was far less nimble and acute than it is normally, and I also noticed that whereas music can normally be sublime to me, it no longer transported me during those weeks, but instead seemed to subtract from rather than add to the already sublime feelings I was enjoying all the time. And the normal pleasures of the company of friends, even of making love, were exceeded by the ineffable pleasures of union with God that solitude made it practicable for me to enjoy during that period.

Often the sublimity of ecstatic experiences and experience of the divine contrasts oddly with external appearances and behaviour. At Cambridge I heard a story of a student who drank too much coffee and worked all night before his examinations, and in the morning announced that he had seen the face of God. Asked to describe his vision, he said "It was just like a molecule of H_2O_2." Similarly, the ecstatic profundity of a satisfying sexual climax is not adequately represented by the spasms, grunts or moans which an outside observer might witness. And if we see a sublime look spreading over the face of a baby we may guess that he is wetting himself or dirtying his nappy. And the baby who is blissfully enjoying the breast is in a state of high vulnerability in relation to the outside world.

The paradoxical nature of these states of subjective harmony and order was vividly borne in upon me in a dream I had some years later. I dreamt of a litter of blind baby mice arranged like the spokes of a wheel, all feeding from a mother or nipple at the centre, and forming a mandala, a symbol prominent at times of subjective unity and order, combining opposites and resolving contradictions, subjectively speaking at least.

The Need for Humour

It is important to preserve a sense of humour about these divine experiences, and to be prepared to admit that my God may appear to you to be simply my infantile omnipotence, split off from my awareness of myself and experienced in an inflated way.

A sense of humour prevents one from being totally possessed by these "non-I" parts of the personality, and it prevents the splitting-off from becoming a fixed feature. Paradoxically, it enables one to avoid heresy and blasphemy and to avoid condemning others as heretical, blasphemous or mad, especially in situations where regression and mass emotions encourage alienation of these parts of the Self. It is a serious, even an evil thing when the sense of humour is lost, and the field of religious experience is one where this may well happen. This is especially so because religious experiences may occur at times of great suffering.

At a time of intense personal suffering, when I was in deep waters, I remember a dream about a god-like, golden, heroic figure who attacked a comedian, destroyed him and threw his body down a sewer. The corpse became a dancing skeleton and a voice said "This is schizophrenia". It is easy to slip into feelings of heroism or genius at these bad times. The theme of the murdered and dismembered hero and of his resurrection are a heritage of our religions, but a psychological attitude involving humour, tolerance and a democratic spirit is, in my opinion, a more recent cultural achievement, and thus more readily lost.

The identification with the god, the loss of humour and the return of the sense of humour in a mad, frightening, reversed form, seems to me to be the epitome of evil, which I regard as an active splitting-off and transformation of the good into its opposite, so that the same libido comes to be used in an opposite way. From the psychological point of view, there are many different forms of alienation and splitting, just as from the moral point of view there are different forms of sin and evil. But again, from a psychological point of view, splitting and dissociation allow life to go on somehow and enable the person to avoid unbearable pain. They may be essential to life and bodily functioning, and to their psychological derivative, the well-being of the "myself".

Just as good and evil are inter-transformable and seem to use the same source of energy in ourselves, so it presumably is with the good God and His opposite.

The Wrath of God

What of the omnipotent, destructive, wrathful, self-centred partisan God of the Old Testament? One can only be sad about this, but to deny this aspect of God, of external reality, and above all of oneself is to court disaster, and to call down thunderbolts from on high.

In my own case the experience of unity, harmony and beneficent inflow which I have described as *the* religious experience of my life was experienced later in more personal ways in relationships with particular people. Naturally there was a tendency to experience loving-father feelings in the course of my personal analysis, in the analytical transference. Some of the omnipotent loving-father attributes of this parental archetype were, as it were, experienced in projection on to the analyst. When the latter inevitably showed his non-loving aspects, I was of course very hurt. On occasions, these shocks of disillusionment were experienced as physical blows. On one occasion I remember the sensation of a severe knock on the head, accompanied by a flash. I regard these shocks as beneficial and the flashes as flashes of insight, or flashes at least resulting eventually in insights.

Apart from these "bolts from the blue", one has to mention the pain of separation, the chastening effects of illness, the blush-making, laxative and releasing results of being found out or of finding oneself out in deceptions and self-deceptions, all these good though unpleasant experiences coming from the "not-I" as well as the experience of the blissful harmony of the divine unity of the Self.

Other Aspects of the Divine

There have been times of potential disillusionment in actual persons who were important to me, when the need to know the actual facts has seemed paramount. This need has on one or two occasions been so compelling and meaningful for a time, that the statement that God is Truth (or Reality) has been the only statement about the Divine that made any sense to me at the time. But then, following the ascertainment of the facts, there may occur a period of understanding and of insight into the subjectively bad aspects of oneself which one had been projecting on to the other person concerned. This sort of insight can be accompanied by beneficial bodily relaxations and unblocking of "body armour" (in the sense of Wilhelm Reich). At such times the statement that "God is Love" seems the most meaningful statement about the Divine that one could make.

So much for my own very ordinary experiences, where it is fairly obvious that the phenomena could well stem from the unconscious, or from a "not-I" part of the Self. I would like to emphasize this with more clinical illustration. An analysand who experienced the power and arbitrariness of God on occasions as a rushing, shattering force, later came to recognize this force as his own rage, hitherto split off from his self-concept (disowned) and experienced passively instead of actively. Schizophrenic patients often demonstrate splitting and projecting in an obvious way, although remaining oblivious of any such split. I had a patient who in a state of acute schizophrenia was utterly beatific while seeing me as the Devil and as a murderer, whenever I was doing or saying something that would in her non-schizophrenic condition have annoyed her considerably. The devilish and murderous feelings were simply and completely projected on to me. She, on the contrary, experienced herself as the embodiment of God's will.

So an "explanation" of God as split-off, omnipotent parts of the Self is sometimes patently true and can surely very often go a long way towards fitting the facts. These split-off portions of the Self are certainly on occasions experienced as objective phenomena by other persons, and it might even be that they materialize.

Matter, Mind and Spirit

It is sometimes easy to demonstrate that a subjective phenomenon like the experience of a mighty rushing wind, or a "bolt from the blue", is due to split-off emotional forces, archetypal in origin no doubt, experienced as "objective". But supposing these ego-alien forces of the Self produce actual material effects, as they probably do in cases of poltergeist activity and of psychokinesis, then we are confronted by the possibility that large-scale natural phenomena, even matter and physical energy themselves, can be treated as ego-alien, potentially psychic events. Such a view of nature could be made philosophically consistent and would complement or even replace a purely materialistic view of "mind". The reader might retort that such a view of matter is simply age-old superstition, and that humankind has paid dearly enough to throw off such shackles. One cannot deny this.

Be all this as it may, these "psychic manifestations" of a material nature seem to yield to ordinary analytic methods which aim at bringing them into relationship with the ego. And interest in them wanes at the same time. But this may be because of the Western ego's ideas about the nature of reality. Our adult Western egos may be alienated from our Selves, from God as a reality which we sometimes glimpse but spend most of our time cutting ourselves off from. We have to admit that it could be so.

But to return to my main point, that an outside observer can often see how my God is simply an unconscious part of myself, I should like to give an example of how this state of affairs is analysed in practice. A devout Oriental patient of mine, who was extremely rich and privileged, did not consciously look after himself and his own interests enough. His aggressions and self-assertion were transformed into somatic illnesses. Although a devout believer, he simply could not see how he himself, or any other single individual, could matter to God among the teeming millions of living and dead people. In other words his God could love humanity in the mass but not as individual people. The patient gave much work and money to people in the mass, and had the utmost difficulty coping deliberately with his own needs. His theological standpoint was not altered by theological argument, but by finding out, through patient analysis of his somatic symptoms and their inter-personal causations, that he mattered to himself, and (therefore, as it were) to God.

Numinous Symbols

Deities and numinous symbols carry intense energy not directly available to the "I", but potentially available for further integration. Numinous symbols lead the "I" on to assimilate more unconscious content, thus enriching itself. The main value of psychotherapy is helping the self-enrichment of the "I" in this assimilative process.

Let me taken an ordinary example of such an enriching process. A patient who had had severe depressive illnesses dreamt in his analysis of a crocodile, a coelecanth and a disc with alternating red and black sectors. In a dream later in analysis the red and black disc changed into a frightening Pan-like face and head. Analysis helped him experience this "devilish" part of himself as (previously repressed) sadistic and satyr-like impulses; analytical work on this aspect of himself helped him become a more lively and free person, far less rigid than formerly. The "devilish" sub-personality was chaotic, whereas the disc had been quite the opposite – geometrical, symmetrical and orderly as a matter of fact. So the Pan-like part of himself had been condensed and transformed into its opposite in the numinous disc symbol and only experienced in projection on to others. Mandala symbols and other numinous symbols may condense, reverse and render harmonious parts of the Self which are at present alien to the "I". The mandala, with its feeling of harmony, of combining opposites, and of order, serves very often to transform and reverse chaotic, destructive and sadistic urges. This may be a reason why mandalas are prominent in connection with non-violent and non-attached Oriental philosophical attitudes (see Chapter 9).

The "devilish" part of my patient had been disallowed in childhood, but a rather violent, bad-tempered streak ran in the family and needed to be understood and used. Insight into this part of himself helped him to become more assertive and less irritable when tired or ill. It does not make one *behave* in a more devilish way. Usually there is a reciprocal relationship between conscious feelings and unconscious acting-out.

Another patient, whose conscious attitude was embittered and misanthropic, had several "visions" of a loving, Christ figure holding out his arms to her. To me, as an observer, the "Christ" part of her was extremely alien to her "I"; many years of analysis away, in fact. But it eventually did become part of her and of her (hitherto abhorring) feelings towards the child in herself.

In conclusion, then, I tend to regard religious experiences, in the first instance at least, as part of the "non-I" part of the Self entering or becoming known to, the "I" part. They therefore connote for me a potential for further self-realization, further restoration of an original unity and in-touchness with oneself and with Reality. This entering may take the form of an implosion, a revelation, a break-through from the not-I, a breakthrough of the I, a volcanic eruption or fountain from the not-I (the unconscious, the depths etc.) into the I, or of a personal, quasi-sexual mystical impregnation or union. The effect is always inflationary but not necessarily pathologically so. It may be enlightening, exciting or ecstatic, but is not necessarily over-stimulating and does not inevitably lead to reactive inhibitory or backlash phenomena, or to epileptoid manifestations. In these states of inflation, which tend to occur at times of personal crisis or emotional disturbance, religious truisms may tend to become personally felt truths. Yet at other times these truths, while remaining meaningful and true, only represent part-truths.

Chapter Four

The omnipotent "I" and the realistic "I"

The polarization in Walter Mitty between his grandiose secret day-dream self and his very ordinary, lesser even than ordinary, real self is a fundamental one with which we all have to struggle at times in our lives; maybe all the time to a certain extent. By taking a few examples from the analytical literature, I intend to show that this polarization exists in psychodynamic psychology, in the differing emphases that different authors may place on the "omnipotent" as opposed to the "realistic" aspects of the self.

Let me begin by comparing the way the psychoanalyst Edith Jacobson (1964) wrote about the self in her book *The Self and the Object World* with the way Jung wrote about the Self. The difference in emphasis is almost complete. Whereas Jacobson's main emphasis was on the development of personal identity based on a realistic self-image, Jung's interest was not primarily in a realistic self-image; he was interested in Self-realization, which in some ways is approaching the problem of finding oneself from the opposite direction to that taken by Jacobson:

> By a realistic self-image we mean, first of all, one that correctly mirrors the state and characteristics, the potentialities and abilities, the assets and limits of our bodily and mental self: on the one hand, of our appearance, our anatomy and our physiology; on the other hand, of our ego, our conscious and pre-conscious feelings and thoughts, wishes, impulses and attitudes, of our physical and mental functions and behaviour (Jacobson, 1964).

Jacobson does acknowledge that "whereas all these single specific aspects will have corresponding psychic representations, a concept of their sum total will simultaneously develop". This awareness of self as separate and distinct from one's environment has continuity and finds emotional expression as the experience of personal identity.

I feel I must interject some comments on Jacobson's approach. Her view of the self is of a sense of separate and individual selfness, of oneself as distinct from the mother or others. It seems to be of a self arising from the *agglomeration of fragments* (of experience of one's body, etc.) and from experiences of separation and differentiation. The outside observer is perfectly free to see the infant developing a realistic self-image in this way. But I do not think it feels like that to the infant. I think that the self-universe (before there is an "I" and "you") may also be experienced subjectively as continuous and in terms of mergings as well as separations, good feelings as well as bad. The bad feelings are pushed away into the discontinuous, at first chaotic not-I world. The archaic experience of person-ness is argued in my article "When are things persons and persons things?" (Redfearn, 1982). But being an analyst of adults I speak without too much confidence about the infant's subjective experience. Mostly when analysts speak of infantile sexuality and archaic ego states they are speaking of regressed adults and not of observable actual infants. The distinction is well worth keeping.

The first year of life is the period when the identity theme, but not yet the identity, is established. Jacobson refers to the processes of incorporation and projection, of fusion with the mother and experiences of separation, of omnipotent and magical control, and so on, in contributing to the theme of identity. She makes no mention of the mother's role in meeting these needs and projections, nor does she mention the way the mother feels about the child and how she relates to it. We know now that the way the mother feels about a child and the way the child perceives her to be seeing him can at least in some cases pretty well determine what the child feels about himself and how the child sees himself.

Jacobson places the discovery of personal identity at about two and a half years. The child gradually develops an ability to distinguish between himself and others. He begins to differentiate between his mother and others in the first year, because of different likelihoods of gratification. Later, rivalry and jealousy play an increasing part in the distinction between self and others.

These selective ego identifications of the normal child, unlike the regressive fusion experiences of the psychotic which are due to object loss because of aggression, cannot be established until the person identified with is experienced both as good and bad, and until love wins out over the hostile, envious, jealous, derogatory feelings. The better the totality of other persons and of the self can be experienced, the more easily can the perception of both likenesses and differences between self and others be tolerated, even desired.

Summarizing Jacobson's views: a person needs a double equipment. On the one hand he needs to live with others in mutual adaptation, mutual gratification and mutual need fulfilment; on the other hand he needs to struggle and fight and assert his freedom as an individual and his right to survive. The initial symbiosis between mother and infant partially continues throughout childhood, and, during or after adolescence is relinquished reluctantly on the part of both parents and child. During childhood there are erratic vacillations between attitudes of passive, helpless dependency on a mother experienced as all-powerful, and active, aggressive strivings for self expansion and the powerful control of the loved objects.

A similar view, which again stresses the omnipotence-foregoing aspects of the mature self, is that of Réne Spitz (1957, pp. 138–9):

> Before he becomes capable of co-ordinating muscular activity volitionally, the child lives in the realm of infantile omnipotence. His desires (needs) were fulfilled by the environment. When there was a delay in the fulfilment, hallucinatory need gratification stepped in. This was possible because reality testing during the first six months of life is practically non-existent. Reality testing is predicated on the availability of perception and motility, both of which are either lacking or inadequately developed during that period.
>
> But when directed intentional muscular co-ordination and after that, around the beginning of the second year, locomotion, is achieved, experience imposes on the child a rapid development of reality testing and reality adaptation. During the transitional period, the mother acts as the protector of the child and teaches him, step by step, to become his own protector and observer. The clash between the child's will and that of the mother leads the child to recognize the limits of his will, his wishes, his phantasies about himself, and thus the boundaries of the self are narrowed and set up. One may say without exaggeration that the self is fashioned from the atrophied remains of magic omnipotence.
>
> This origin of the self, its linkage with magic omnipotence, will never be completely eradicated and can be traced even in the adult. Reality testing blocks the road of return to the omnipotent origin of the self.

Jacobson and Spitz, at least in the quotations I have selected, seem to be writing very much from the point of view of the grown-up part of ourselves observing the child from outside. The emphasis is practical, realistic (i.e. external reality), sensible and omnipotence-foregoing.

Let me contrast this emphasis with that of Neumann in his book *The Child*. He says

> A normally positive primal relationship results on the one hand in an attitude of confidence toward the human environment and one's own body, and on the other hand in unquestioning confidence in the Self. Such confidence is indespensable to the stability of the ego-Self axis which is the spinal cord of individual automorphism and, later on, of a stable ego and ego-consciousness (Neumann, 1973/1976, p. 43).

Here the emphasis is on a confident stable self rather than on a realistic self-image. Winnicott (1965) also, in his distinction between the true self of the infant and the compliant false self, seems to empathize with the "omnipotent" child rather than the demands of grown-up reality. He calls the reality-oriented self a healthy, mild degree of false self and says

> In health, the false self is represented by the whole organization of the polite and mannered social attitude, a "not wearing the heart on the sleeve", as might be said. Much has gone to the individual's ability to forego omnipotence and the primary process in general, the gain being the place in society which can never be attained or maintained by the True Self alone (Winnicott, 1965, p. 143).

Speaking of the mother's part in the degree of harmony or disharmony between true and false self, Winnicott continues (p. 145):

> The good-enough mother meets the omnipotence of the infant and to some extent makes sense of it. She does this repeatedly . . . A true self does not become a living reality except as a result of the mother's repeated success in meeting the infant's spontaneous gesture or sensory hallucination . . . that is made real . . . the capacity of the infant to *use a symbol* is the result.
>
> The mother who is not good enough is not able to implement the infant's omnipotence, and so she repeatedly fails to meet the infant gesture; instead, she substitutes her own gesture which is to be given sense by the compliance of the infant. This compliance on the part of the infant is the first stage of the false self.
>
> The true self comes from the aliveness of the body tissues and the working of body functions, including the heart's action and breathing. It is closely linked with the primary process, and is, at the beginning, essentially not reactive to external stimuli, but primary. There is little point in formulating a true self idea except for the purpose of trying to understand the false self, because it does no more than collect the details of the experience of aliveness (ibid., p. 148).
>
> In between the infant and the object (mother or part of the mother-present author) is some thing, or some activity or sensation. In so far as this joins the infant to the object . . . so far is this the basis of symbol formation. On the other hand, in so far as this something separates instead of joins, so is its function of leading on to symbol-formation blocked (ibid., p. 146).

Let me now go back to the quotation from Spitz to the effect that "Reality testing blocks the road of return to the omnipotent origin of the self". My quotation from Winnicott prompts me to remark that there are differing kinds of reality. There is the reality which joins us to our good, loved, external and internal "persons" and does not block but on the contrary opens up the road of return to our "infantile omnipotence" and thus to life. This kind of reality would have symbolic value in Jung's sense. Good management ensures that reality does not cut off the other person (child, patient, employee, subordinate, enemy etc.) from his omnipotence. In the field of therapist–child relationships, the following quotation from a case of Michael Fordham (1957) illustrates this point.

Fordham is describing a schizoid boy who is angrily threatening the analyst with an omnipotent monster – Jungian Self, Winnicottian true self. The monster was also a dot. Fordham continues:

> One day the child became very insistent on the subject of whether I knew God before I was inside my mother's stomach when I was a dot inside God . . . When at length I interpreted this insistence as being his wish to be sure that I could not contradict him if he asserted that he knew God in reality, a change occurred in his whole demeanour and he poured out a long and elaborate series of *ex cathedra* thoughts which expressed mental concepts of the following kind: "Because there is something there must be nothing", or "Spirits are nothing because they can go through you and you can stick things through them – but that is something."
>
> He was thinking in terms of opposites, and behind these thoughts lay a psychical dynamic which expressed itself in a cosmology of fairies, witches, devils, and a god. Interspersed with this there gradually developed evidence of positive ego functioning, for the child was able to explain how he felt and to relate his feelings to the present and other situations. For instance, going away from my room presented a difficulty, since at this point his feeling of omnipotence was threatened (Fordham, 1957, p. 144).

I include this quotation from Fordham because it seems to me that here the analyst was successfully meeting the child's omnipotence in that the "true self" did not have to remain hidden, as it had been, and the omnipotent defence could be replaced by a personal relationship with an acknowledgement of dependence. I now quote from my own notes the case of a schizophrenic young woman during an acute episode when she had to be kept inside a closed ward for her own safety. At this time she was continually hallucinated; mostly it was God she was in communication with. My notes for one interview at that time read as follows:

> 6.9.67. When I entered her room she told me not to close the door as there was a conspiracy. Wanted to be put in a proper hospital. Looked dehydrated, said she could not eat or drink because of the poison. When I said something to the effect of my being a bad mummy she said that was just analytical talk, she really was being poisoned. I said she was so angry that I had not said I was in love with her she was denying many real unpleasant things. She started muttering about being in communication with God, who was still in the same place in her head. She got out of bed, told me to hold a spoon in front of me and she would get us out. I did so; she went to the door and started to pray. Sure enough the nurse opened the door of the room from the outside! (The door could not be opened from the inside.)
>
> She went out saying, "Let us go away together". I followed. When she was going out of the hospital door I called her sharply back. She looked at me with venom and said "You devil". However, she walked back into the hospital. She walked into the sterilizer room of the ward and I followed. She said: "Shall we open the window?" I said it could not be opened. She picked up a tin and was about to smash the window. However, I quickly got it away from her and said "Naughty girl" sharply and spontaneously. Shortly after that it was time for me to go. I asked a nurse to stay with her and told her I would be back tomorrow. As I left she called after me "Daddy" with such real feeling that I was moved to go back to her, squeeze her hand, and say again that I would return tomorrow.

I include these case notes because the patient was at that time illustrating most of the points raised by Jacobson, Spitz and Winnicott, and I was having some of the problems that a parent has in, as Winnicott has it, meeting her omnipotence – a delightfully vague expression but not I think quite covering the head-on clashes we were having at that time, when I perforce found myself strongly and emotionally involved on the side of "commonsense reality" and of Winnicott's "false self", perhaps. Later when she was no longer psychotic she used to say that her voices of God were "all wrong" so that I then found myself on the side of the voices, i.e. of the "true self".

My aim in this chapter has been, by citing typical authoritative authors, to delineate one important dimension along which authors' emphases tend to polarize. Some authors, such as Searles and Winnicott, tend to emphasize the importance of the mother or the therapist in meeting the omnipotent needs of the infant or patient in the building of self-confidence and in eventual self-realization. Others, such as Spitz and Jacobson, emphasize the ability of the healthy child to forego omnipotence and build up a realistic self-image. Jung himself could be regarded as a pioneer in the approach to the primal self as the source of energy and life, but he was equally aware of the importance of separation and differentiation from the parental imagos in the process of individuation.

A "Jungian" author who has demonstrated the use by children of symbols of the self is Michael Fordham (1957). Fordham's "primal self" is an original, boundaryless, cosmic, timeless state of being or experience, an original wholeness or integrate.

Fordham's primal self and Jacobson's primal psycho-physiological self both seem to refer to an initial undifferentiated state of being endowed with undifferentiated drive energy. From this energy Jacobson derives both libidinal and aggressive strivings while leaving the possibility open for other drives such as hunger, which, she points out, has no place in current psychoanalytic theory. Fordham's model, while not attempting to describe or enumerate the basic human drives, allows for a multiplicity of instinctual and stimulus–response patterns down to the spinal level. The functioning of these basic behaviours is termed by Fordham de-integration, referring to a division in the primary integrate of the self when such basic behaviours occur. An example of such a basic pattern would be suckling behaviour. These early behaviours and bodily patterns and impulses may subjectively be endowed with a cosmic or boundariless quality, partaking of some of the qualities of the primary Self integrate.

Jacobson makes very little use of the primal psycho-physiological self as a source of integration or of energy, whereas to the Jungian view the Self underlies and affects everything. Jacobson is on firmer ground when referring to the self-image. This is defined as "the unconscious, pre-conscious and conscious endo-psychic representation of the bodily and mental self within the system ego". In practice this may be taken to refer to one's self-concept and one's awareness of oneself in one's body. The energetic or drive resources of this self suffer from the usual psychoanalytic paucity and rigidity. The Jungian notion of archetypes and archetypal energies, sub-personalities, deriving ultimately, by de-integration, from the primal Self, seems to be lacking. At the same time it must be admitted that the importance of what might be called healthy narcissistic needs and the clinical phenomenology of narcissistic personality disorders are matters which have been pioneered more by psychoanalysts than by Jungian authors. The grandiose and omnipotent needs of the individual human being receive detailed and sensitive attention in the works of Winnicott, Searles and Kohut. The Jungian Self, with its positive view of so-called "symptoms" and "abnormalities", also gives due respect to this "unrealistic" side of the human person, as does the whole concept of the Jungian Self.

It is possible that in our culture there is a "generation-gap" between the "grown-up" and the "infantile" parts of ourselves which causes an unnecessary and damaging split between omnipotence and realism, between spirit and matter eventually and results in our philosophical polarizations. If we are divided from our childish selves, we cannot meet the omnipotent demands and the narcissistic satisfactions and frustrations which our children need in order to build selves in which omnipotence and realism are compatible with each other.

Jacobson's "realistic self-image" corresponds rather closely to Jung's persona–shadow pair of opposites. When we analyse the persona, Jung (1945) says in "The relations between the ego and the unconscious", there comes a moment when the subject experiences the feeling of "god-likeness", which announces itself by means of peculiarities of the body image. He may dream he is flying through space like a comet, or feel that he is the earth, the sun or a star, that he is immense or extremely small, that he is too short, too tall or too big for his skin, or that he is falling or rising endlessly, and he may feel vertiginous and disorientated. He may at this time be unusually vulnerable to physical illness. The analogy between this phase of analysis and mental disorder is almost complete. But there is no actual insanity unless the contents of the unconscious become a reality which usurp the place of conscious reality.

In other words, the dissolution of the persona corresponds with the dissolution of the false self, the break-through of omnipotence and the break-up of the stable reality-based body-image. The dissolution of the persona, Jung says, positively invites one to plunge into the ocean of divinity and, losing all memory, to merge oneself with it. This propensity is the wish to fuse with the mother.

In "normal" development the reverse occurs and we now know more about the dates when these developments take place. But it is clear that these processes are happening in either direction throughout life. The precursors of the I/not-I dichotomy are the mental representations of the processes of ingestion and ejection and the fantasies of incorporation and expulsion based on them. Bad feelings are ejected from the "I", good feelings incorporated into the "I". Spitz places the I/not-I dichotomy at nine months and self-awareness at fifteen months. Complete muscular and bowel control and growing independence proceed through the second year. At two to two and a half years, Jacobson says, one can say "I am me" with a real sense of pleasure and individuality.

Fordham has shown that the ability to draw a circle in one child occurred at just over a year and preceded the learning of the word "I". When the child started to say "I" the circle-drawing stopped. He also described (Fordham, 1957, p. 135) a two and a half-year-old girl whom he asked to sit on his knee and draw. She first drew angry scribbles and finally a circle, after which she happily got down from his knee and went off. Thus the circle meant "I can wish, and hope, and feel that it is safe to be a separate individual". Fordham related this to what he called the ego developing out of the matrix of the self. In the terminology I am using, it would be the "I"-representation arising out of the matrix of the primal self. The circle does not simply mean "I am foregoing omnipotence"; it means "it is safe because I am containing omnipotent rage and not projecting it on to my environment". Fordham's handling enabled this to happen.

In Jung's memoirs the symbols of the giant, man-eating phallus, the black manikin with his good-and-bad turdstone, the God who destroyed the cathedral with his turd and the round, shimmering jelly-fish were all emergent aspects of the Self. They were all split-off parts of himself acting as foci for subsequent expansion of consciousness of his I-feeling.

His main work on the self was a struggle to realize these omnipotent parts of himself without losing contact with reality. His struggle is in this sense taking place in all of us.

Chapter Five

The body, the body-image and the self

What are the essential connections between myself, my bodily self, my body as I experience it, and my physical body as studied in the physiological laboratory and the dissecting room? The psychotherapist's work occupies a key position in beginning to provide an answer in human, practical terms. The philosopher, the academic psychologist and the medical scientist each provide very partial and one-sided answers, fascinating though they may be. The main purpose of this book is to contribute to the kind of perspective which is necessary.

Scientific medicine may have helped to cut us off from actually experiencing our bodies, certainly in so far as bodily experiences are related to feelings and emotions. Certainly the medical approach and the medical curriculum in my experience helped to cut off bodily experience from oneself, and to replace the body as experienced subjectively with the body as discovered by the physiologist and the anatomist. Before Harvey discovered the mechanism of the circulation of the blood, Western medicine, like all the medicines before and all other medical systems, seems to have had a close relationship with our bodies as we actually experience them, but since the era of scientific medicine the actual body and the body of actual experience have been cut off from each other. Psychosomatic medicine hopes to re-establish the connection, as do Oriental medicine, Reichian and humanistic psychologies, but in this book I am trying to deal with the connection that we as human individuals manage to make with our own bodies and feelings and the connection between self-confidence, narcissism and bodily experience, between "thinking" and "feeling" etc.

In order to make clear the distinction between the body as experienced by me and as related to feelings as opposed to the body as studied in scientific medicine, I should like to describe the experience of a patient of mine who was suffering from influenza during an epidemic of that disease. One night, when the disease was at its height, he lay awake, tossing about restlessly, with sore throat and aching limbs. It occurred to him that a hot drink might help him get to sleep. Having a fever, he knew that if he got up to make one himself he would be shivering violently and feeling wretched. But his wife was asleep and he did not wish to trouble her, so he decided after all to get up himself. Naturally enough he felt a bit noble and a bit sorry for himself as he began to prepare the drink. His nose and eyes began to run profoundly and he started to sneeze. As he sneezed and sneezed and as his eyes watered and watered he experienced something very meaningful to him (this is the point of my story). He had a strong feeling of once again being an abandoned child weeping noisily. His running eyes and nose did not merely represent or symbolize tears, they *were* tears to him at that moment in a sense that felt very profound and meaningful to him. The attack of influenza itself acquired a meaning at the same time in the same terms (i.e. as a regression). As he sipped his hot drink in bed afterwards he felt the experience had been a very enriching one. It gave him new insights into his tendency to overwork (necessitating periodical regressions), into the reasons for this, insights into his relationship with his wife as "mother", and a better, more emphatic understanding of his wife and her problems – it brought him closer to her.

When he told me about this experience and his reflections, I remarked that it all made very good sense to me and that I was interested that he seemed to have left the influenza virus out of the picture completely in his understanding of his illness. He agreed and said he knew all about the role of the influenza virus, but he hardly ever caught these infections, and he thought the essential meaning of his illness was as he had described. The experience had helped him make sense of his life at the time and in any case this was what mattered.

In contrasting the body as felt and experienced meaningfully and the body as described by scientific medicine, I am of course not being at all fair to modern medicine, which professes to take full account of the patient as a person (but which has insufficient time to do so in practice). But what mattered to my patient was that the experience had helped him to relate more meaningfully, more richly, with his body, his self and self-feelings, his work and way of life and even with his wife and what he expected of her.

This is what I mean by a meaningful working relationship between the "I" and bodily experience. The relationship works through feelings, personal relationships and through the meaning and meaningfulness of one's bodily experiences. My patient was getting in touch with his body image of feeling and emotional expression, the body image as it is described by the poets, as it expresses itself in body language, and as it can be experienced and expressed coanaesthetically, i.e. with all the senses and bodily impulses at once. This is the body image of feeling and of a meaning that can be heard musically, danced, painted, written down in poetry or related to other people and their effect on oneself. It is the body-image that is "projected" on to other people and on to one's reconstruction of the world. Rather than referring to it merely as "body-image" or "body-schema", I should prefer to call it "the coanaesthetic body-world schema of affective experience". This is too cumbersome to use all the time but it is usually what I mean when I refer to "body-image" or "body-world schema".

This body-world schema must exist in potentia from the beginning of life. Just as what goes on in a community of humans or animals affects each member of that community, so what goes on in one part of an organism affects what goes on in each part of it. Furthermore, once a nervous system is established, the whole organism comes to be represented topographically at various levels in the hierarchy of functions in the nervous system. Each level of the nervous system carries a more or less faithful map of the whole organism, as it were. The body-world schema, then, does not suddenly exist when consciousness or self-awareness is established, but is in the most simple case another way of talking about the primary integrative functions of the organism.

In adult life, this body-world schema is approached through feeling and through the world of poetry and metaphor as far as verbal language is concerned. In my opinion, it is the basis of the primary integrate and of the primary integrative functions, as well as of the later "I", and of a normal sort of personal identity. The "realistic" self-image and the "self-concept" of conscious experience are much more partial and are secondary matters.

The feeling of "I" usually dwells in the body-image, often in Western Man in the head part of it. Certain parts of our bodies or, more accurately, their corresponding representations in the body-image may be permanently or temporarily cut off and unavailable to the feeling of "I". Parts of ourselves which are ill or give rise to anxiety are often the target for alienating processes of this sort. They become much more "not-I" than they are normally, and behave like other persons who are enemies or who have to be nursed etc. Or they may even become "things" rather than "persons", although this would be a result of a rather severe degree of depersonalization.

In the case of the influenza patient, his love for his wife, and his willingness to suffer a certain amount of trouble for her sake, enabled him to experience the feelings which connected his bodily experience with his past and with the mother-image. But there is a level of mental functioning which precedes this stage of concern for the other as a separate person, whether we call this level an unconscious level of functioning, as Jungians might, or a paranoid–schizoid level, as Kleinians might.

At this earlier level, "evil" is synonymous with bad bodily feelings and "goodness" with good body feelings. At this earlier stage, projection of badness into others or into the environment is necessary for bodily health. Let me give an example of this, a case I shall call the "healthy young man" (very much in quotes of course). In this narcissistic young man, bodily health depended on such defences as these.

The body of the "healthy young man" seemed to be to an unusual degree in charge of his "I". He gave the impression of glowing health. He experienced himself as like a potentially beautiful tree whose growth was continually being threatened or stunted by inimical and arbitrary authority figures. In analysis, after a honeymoon period, there was a phase of intense physical and mental suffering during which he gradually became more realistic. The sessions were now largely spent pouring out abuse at me and the others. This release of bad feelings made him feel better, whereas I often felt weak or depressed after them. I was usually allowed to say very little, but what I did say, even if such was not my intention, often made it clear to him that I did not take the same view of the situation as did he, and that I felt he was leaving himself out as a contributory factor in the bad things that were always happening to him. When I did manage to say something, I felt better, and he worse. He would be unable to sleep and would suffer from headaches, vomiting, sensations of being crushed, of hard masses in his body, of being gashed etc. In his sleepless state he would be compelled to work over in his mind the monstrous and unfair things I had said to him that day, until he had in some way, by some reasoning, vanquished me in his mind. He would then, and only then, be able to sleep. He would awake refreshed and able to fit what I had said into his scheme of things, with his (to my mind) paranoid defences restored. His body was now restored, and his mind illuminated by the revelations he had been vouchsafed during the night. On waking he would make copious notes of his conclusions to present at the next session. To me these were a dreary repetition, with almost imperceptible variations, of the basic and perpetual persecutory theme.

In this phase of our work, which lasted well over a year, my interpretations, which were partly attempts at self-preservation on my part, were experienced as bodily as well as narcissistic wounds by him. After most sessions he needed to restore his paranoid defences and his bodily well-being, by conscious mental activity and by dreamwork of a similar sort, with concomitant experiences of mental illumination. The Schreber diaries (Schreber, 1903), on which Freud based his exposition of his theory of paranoia, contain numerous examples of the same phenomenon.

On the other hand, with patients who in the course of analysis become physically ill, there is often a need to maintain certain idealizations (say, of mother-representation in the psyche, or of feelings about an actual mother), so that the bad feelings are directed at the self, which, at this level, equals the body feelings and the body-image. My experience extends to several patients of this sort, including two or three serious illnesses. The important connection between narcissism, the mother figure, the body-image and the "real" body of the dissecting room cannot be doubted after experiences like these. The illness or self-destructive act represents an attack on the bad mother/self and an attempt to preserve the idealized mother-image.

I have contrasted the influenza victim with the "healthy young man" because the former had a creative and aware way of experiencing his body (and everything else for that matter) which the latter did not have. What was missing in the "healthy young man" was what Jung referred to as the "symbolic attitude", an attitude of penetrating deeper than the concrete external facts and reaching inner, psychic truths. The "revelations" of the "healthy young man" often contained flamboyant religious and archetypal imagery, but were only used to confirm him in his bodily well-being and his feeling of being right. The influenza victim could love in a way the "healthy young man" could not love. He could suffer for others and also in his own best interests.

Transformations of Narcissistic Libido

As I have said, much of what I said to the "healthy young man" during one phase of his analysis was a severe narcissistic impingement upon him. Narcissistic impingements may be good as well as bad and may be experienced as bodily sensations in various parts of the body. They may also vary in their quality and differentiatedness, and in the degree of somatic effect. One of the chief determinants is of course the feelings towards the person producing the impingement.

In analysis we are often in a position to observe the vicissitudes of narcissistic libido. Bodily feelings or bodily symptoms often change or reverse during the course of analysis. Erotic excitement, for example, may produce good bodily feelings at one time and bad body feelings at another, depending on whether the excitement or the erotic fantasy is occurring under the auspices of the Good Mother archetype or of the Terrible Mother. I recall a patient who when masturbating on his own to the accompaniment of sadistic fantasies, usually had a delicious warm feeling in his abdomen. However, when erotic fantasies were activated in my presence, forbidding parent as I represented to him, he had severe pains in the same area of his body. There was a reversal of bodily libido sign as a result of the change of auspices.

Changing the sign of bodily sensations of this kind may take a long time, but reversal may also occur rapidly in either direction as the "auspices" reverse or alter, i.e. as love or negative feelings predominate. The outward flow of libido is very difficult to stop: it is more easily reversed in sign than direction. We all know how a person whose heart and soul are in a particular activity or personal relationship gets into real trouble if the activity or the person ceases to exist or to be available. He may regress, become ill, depressed or hypochondriacal. He may sleep it off. There may be an activation of mental imagery, perhaps of a primordial type. Wise counsel at such times can be life-saving. As far as bodily well-being is concerned, it seems to matter little whether the outwardly directed energy is love, hate or work – hence the efficacy of revenge for the loss of a loved one, as far as "feeling better" or even actual bodily health are concerned. Much therapy, magic, ritual and prayer works by reversing or deflecting the flow of libido and by finding outlets for it, but analysis seeks to do more than this.

Relationship between One's Actual Body and the Representation of the Mother's Body

There is an important unconscious equation between one's own body-in-action and "the mother's body" of unconscious fantasy (usually the Great Mother archetype of Jungian psychology). This, I believe, should be regarded as the First Law of Psychosomatics, analogous with the First Law of Thermodynamics in physics. My next clinical example illustrates a change of auspices of the kind I was describing in the last section, but it also introduces the idea of the way this law operates in practice.

This man was hypochondriacal and often in fact really ill. He had been brought up by a dominating mother who often combined with his elder brother against him. He had married a dominating wife who often compared him unfavourably with other men. He had several bodily afflictions when he first saw me, including chronic colitis, with blood or mucus in the stools. He had a strong fear of cancer as well as other bodily fears. When he found himself able to pour out his feelings, both good and bad, to me, I became a powerful ally in his mind, and so he now lived, as it were, under the auspices of a powerful supportive parent rather than those of a denigrating parent. Under this "change of auspices" there occurred a marked diminution in his various symptoms, and a beginning of intensely creative artistic activity (which has since continued) as opposed, perhaps, to the psychological and painful bowel affliction which previously caused him so much distress. The artistic creativity began after a dream in which a man with cancer of the bowels was cured when a jewel, probably a diamond, was placed in the middle of the tumour. At this time in his therapy he began to make confident and well-reasoned verbal attacks on his wife. He now felt with certainty that he and his powerful ally, myself, were in the right and she in the wrong. The image of cancer, I believe, could be said to represent his wish to attack the bad mother. Thus his own body, the body-image of the hypochondriacal fantasy, was being attacked by the cancer and was being used as an object of the cancerous hatred "instead" of the mother's body being attacked, as we say. "Instead" or not, the mother's (fantasy) body and his own body-image are closely identified with each other in practice, as always is the case with an attacker and his victim. The diamond and his artistic creativity symbolize and represent a reversal of the cancerous hatred, and it is important, no doubt, that the jewel has been placed in the centre of the cancer by some therapeutic, outside agency. I was acting as a good impregnator-father and a sympathetic recipient of his outpourings at the time. This sort of therapeutic transformation under a "change of auspices" is common enough in therapy, but it is not what one means by analysis as it does not deal with the twin problem of idealization and paranoid projections.

This level of confusion or identity between one's own body-image and the fantasy image of the mother's, or rather the Mother's, is the psychosomatic level proper, I think. I have often found that what the patient's actual, somatic body is *really* doing (quite split off from conscious awareness or at least from the effective "I"), this is what the Mother of his fantasy is, in fantasy, doing to him. Thus a patient whose actual body is vomiting often dreams or images that a parent figure, or society etc., is vomiting him in some sense – ejecting, or rejecting or being disgusted by, him. In an exactly analogous way a schizophrenic patient, while crumpling up a piece of paper in his hand, may have the delusory fantasy or some hallucinatory experience to the effect that he is himself being crushed by some immense force or divine hand. We have the same reversal or confusion between subject and object in both cases, and the same sort of "splitting" defence.

The Pre-I and Non-I Level of Bodily Experience

Bodily impulses and body sensations tend to transcend in experience the boundaries of what is subjectively felt as the "myself". This is not just the case with infants and psychotic patients, although it is most clearly observed in such persons.

I am speaking of instances where impulses of or from the body are experienced not as contained in the personal myself-in-my-body but in projection (on to the mother or her representative) or as boundaryless forces, for example as winds, floods, fires, earthquakes or their good paradaisal counterparts. This is the level where bodily drives and impulses are experienced coenaesthetically as boundaryless or cosmic events. Thus a patient whose wife is metaphorically his whole world may dream of earthquakes or great fires if she has been angry with him. To integrate this amount of anger, and take responsibility for it, is a long, long way away from the capacities of his "I". In analysis, the analyst's ability to feel and meet feelings of this level of experience is crucial. From this the patient learns how it can be done. At this level actual body equals cosmos, world parent, Great Mother.

At a later stage, the impulses may be represented by someone or something with a body. This is progress towards containment and body-identity. For example, a black snake appeared quite frequently at one phase of analysis of an elderly woman patient of mine. It wrapped itself round houses etc, and to her it was associated with the people in her life who clung dependently to her and restricted her life. Only after a few months did she recognize in the snake her own (hitherto rejected) "bad" clinging feelings with their powerful erotic component – her wishes to wrap herself around the analyst in his aspect of mother. This self-image – of the black, enwrapping snake – is the opposite of her usual persona, that of a high-powered, professional, caring and responsible person. The snake impulse was experienced coanaesthetically during the time when she was assuming responsibility for it. It could be painted, danced, described in poems and experienced as a bodily impulse towards me in the therapy, as she lay on the couch, wanting to reach out to me. All this helped to make contact with the feeling of the snake and what it meant to her; gradually the phase of the snake was replaced by succeeding phases of the analysis. But the experience of the snake as self-image is usually an important one in integrating bodily impulses and "lower" levels of the self, previously repudiated.

Such a self image often conflicts with the previous persona of the patient, and at this stage disturbances of the normally experienced body image are common. There may be changes in subjective size, floating feelings, spontaneous rhythmical activity of the trunk, god-like feelings or depersonalization. All these are a result of the previously "non-I" parts of the self irrupting into the "I-in-my-body". Bodily illness may also occur at this stage. At this level, verbal, reductive analysis takes second place to caring management and continued personal meetings. I am using the term persona here to mean the hitherto preferred, or habitual, self-image, or the habitual way of presenting to oneself or the world, e.g. a caring, independent, supportive persona in this case.

It is highly probable that the tendency in a person to experience given primal emotions as extra-personal forces would depend largely on the real mother's original ability to meet, contain and validate her own and her infant's emotions in the early months of the life of the person in question. Certainly the analyst's ability to experience these archetypal forces sympathetically in the analytical relationship determines whether these primal impulses and emotions are to remain alienated or whether they eventually become integrated into the "I" of the analysand, and personal responsibility taken for them (see Newton and Redfearn, 1977).

If most channels of physical communication with the mother are blocked, the remaining ones may become overcharged with significance or feeling or they may be idealized. The mother of one of my patients had been able to cure his headaches with what felt like a divine touch of her hand. In adult life he usually became violently angry if his wife did not feel inclined for love when he felt so moved. If he attempted to contain and restrain the expression of his annoyance, his body would feel "turned to stone". He felt tense and experienced rheumatic pains in the joints. Bodily well-being and relaxation could be restored if he embraced his wife in a mutually loving experience or, alternatively, if he expressed his anger. Yet another possible reaction was to sulk and withdraw into a quiet, understanding, self-contained state, out of which he would gradually emerge over a period of hours or days.

All these reactions are everyday and commonplace reactions to frustration in desire and in attempts at communication. The concept of libido being blocked, directed, reversed (love turning to anger, anger against the mother turned to anger against the self) and so on is a useful, experience-near one, but soon becomes inadequate if taken too seriously as a theoretical construct. The paths along which "libido" may flow and be transformed is the world of the archetypes, of the relationships between the archetypes, and thus are described by the myths of mankind, or by the dramas of everyday life and stage. Nothing less complex is adequate, but simplified schemata of these transformations can justifiably be worked out.

Transposition and Superposition of Parts within the Body-world Schema

Suppose a patient dreams of a person (a witch or a Punch-like figure) with a long, phallic nose. The analyst may feel that intrusive, nosey-parker impulses or fantasies in the transference–countertransference relationship and in the patient's early relationships, might be worth exploring with the patient. Suppose that a patient brings up the image of a unicorn. We might feel that phallic, piercing or penetrative, aspects of the head – the mind or the intellect perhaps – are worth looking at. In other words, the dream image is useful in the first place as an important aspect of the self-image and its projection on to others. The combination of body parts in a symbol represents a combination or superimposition of differing impulses, differing behaviour patterns. Similarly, a dream about a lighthouse is not just a dream about a phallus, but it is probably about an "illuminating phallus", a phallus as teacher or bringer of awareness and so forth. The same considerations apply to different kinds of holes and containers. The kind of container may tell us something about the ways in which the mother-as-container has become experienced and the containing-impulses experienced and transformed (see Redfearn, 1982).

The common superpositions of bodily impulses and drives are often represented as commonly occurring compound dream images and commonly occurring mythological creatures or types of person. Interpretation is usually suggested by considerations of this sort. Sometimes bizarre distortions of the body image occur, e.g. a penis-like growth attached to the back or abdomen. Here we may well have to look at displacements and avoidances. For example, a woman patient dreaming of a tumour on her back followed this with a dream of having a penis in the usual place.

Other common distortions of the body image involve strains and stretching and disfigurations of a surreal quality. These distortions, either of shape or colour, always in my experience indicate how the person feels in himself or about himself. Similarly, images of mutilation, castration, hanging, decapitation etc. always indicate not what the patient fears may happen so much as what is actually happening all the time with that particular patient. For example, a hanged figure may represent a serious block or inhibitory zone separating body-feeling from head-feeling. Such blocks may, interestingly enough, be reflected in bands of tension or paraesthesia in the actual body of the patient, changes which may be approachable and modifiable through massage and other approaches to the actual body. Such approaches are not usually practicable in analysis itself, as they are too highly charged with transference (incest etc.) affects to be readily integrated into analytical work, or else, if not experienced consciously, the affect is split off together with the transference elements.

Dreams involving dismemberment or of isolated bodily parts, similarly, indicate splitting defences whereby the part in question is alienated, split off, from the "I", the main part of the body. Holding and containing by the analyst may produce healing experiences of coming together and wholeness. Dismemberments and splits of this sort are, ontologically, among the most primitive of negative feelings, but this should not necessarily lead us to conclude that the feeling of self and image of oneself arises out of the accretion of images of bodily fragments, or of islands of consciousness coming together or any other kind of agglomerative process.

Migration of "I"-feeling

The "I" in dreams is usually much more mobile than is the feeling of "I" in waking life. The observer in the dream may be outside the subject's body and normal persona, or it may be divided between people. But, to a lesser extent, the waking "I" is subject to migrations within the body and outside it. "Empathy" obviously involves such a migration of the "I", or partial migration. Some of the phenomena of depersonalization involve migrations of "I" feeling, or loss of "I" feeling from its normal location within the body image. This sort of phenomenon suggests that "I"-feeling, with its close association with awareness, consciousness and will, is correlated with some sort of neural excitatory process occurring as a locus or focus of excitation in a sheet or multidimensional mass of nerve cells subserving the body-world schema.

The body-world scheme is experienced in dreams as a landscape or "world", an aspect of the Great Mother (mother earth). As I have said, this is a psychic level at which the "I" is not differentiated from the "thou", the mother. The landscape therefore reflects the actual body in so far as this is represented in the parts of the nervous system subserving mental representations. It is in this sense an image of the Self. If I dream of making a journey, we are dealing with a migration of the "I" feeling into different regions of the Self – at a level where self-feeling actual body and mother image are not differentiated. If the landscape consists of underground caves or containers, we should not try in our interpretations to distinguish between a representation of one's own fantasy insides or the mother's insides or fantasy insides, because we are at a psychic level where the distinction is not made.

As the "I" makes its journey into different regions of the "personality" or of the "body-world scheme" or the World Mother, it encounters representations of various sub-personalities. These may be persons, animals, landscape features, aids or obstacles. Jung's work has demonstrated a tendency towards circular motions and a tendency towards a notion of a centre and an aim or goal. In waking life we have the same notion in one's purpose in life and in the notion of personal aims. After all, journeys and migrations are usually made in order to get somewhere or to get away from something. We can say that, empirically, we find that the goal represents both one's highest aim, one's deepest regression, and the centre of the not-I. More of this will I hope become clear in the final chapters of this book. In the meantime, the reader may care to look at Bunyan's journey, Dante's discoveries, quests for the elusive holy or therapeutic object, and geographical and scientific explorations in the way suggested in this section, if he has not already been in the habit of so doing.

Chapter Six

Are our "minds" in our heads? The location of the feeling of "I"

This chapter concerns "the mind" as a subjective experience or experience-near concept, especially as it is used in such expressions as "losing one's mind" or "blowing one's top". In such metaphors, a close relationship between conscious control and the "head" part of the body-world scheme is often implied.

In regressions and in states of subjectively experienced possession of the "I" by normally "not-I" parts of the self, there is often a partial or complete loss of the feeling of control by the "I". I find that in clinical investigations of such states the patient very often describes sensations in the head just before or when the regression or "possessed" state occurs. In this chapter I shall give a few examples of typical changes and add some speculations about the significance of such observations.

Before I do this I should like once more to stress the distinction between the actual anatomical body of the dissecting room and the body as experienced subjectively. In the case of my kidneys, for example, I know from my medical studies and even perhaps from X-rays and other investigations that they actually exist, but I have virtually no subjective experience of them as kidneys in the body-world scheme of my subjective experience. Perhaps I may have particular pains which I am told or know are due to renal pathology, but again that is not the same thing. But in the case of my mind I have a great deal of subjective experience which I refer to "my mind" and most people in our culture experience it as having some relationship with the "head" part of their bodily experiences. If I say "my heart sank", I am again referring to a real bodily sensation, but its relationship with my actual anatomical heart is a subject of speculation and research rather than of direct observation. But if I say "my heart missed a beat", I am describing an anatomical event as well as a subjective experience. Similarly, when a baby twiddles his fingers and sees as well as feels them moving, two schemata come into tangential relationship. Bringing one's various body-world schemata into apposition and consistency between themselves is one way of describing mental life.

If I say "What you just said cut through me like a knife" I am describing actual bodily experience and such descriptions often tally with the actual wish or fantasy of the other person – in this case a wish or need to make a cutting attack on me. The analyst uses these subjective experiences of his own to provide data on the unconscious fantasies of the analysand which when compared with dream material and actual behaviours of the analysand go towards the building up of interpretative work.

It is probable that subjective experiences of free flowing or streamings in the body, and experiences of blockages and tensions, formed the basis of primitive physiological systems and pre-scientific anatomical schemata involving vapours and humours.

In everyday life most people I have questioned locate their minds inside their heads. We use the word "mind" both in a qualitative sense, for example differentiating "mind" from "heart" and "soul", and in a kind of quantitative sense, in differentiating voluntarily directed thinking from daydreaming. One is more likely to get a thick head from going round a museum trying to absorb things into one's mind, than from day-dreaming, and this is subjectively linked with having "used one's mind" more. Again, most people of the dozens I have questioned locate their feeling of "me" or "I" most strongly in their heads, although many locate themselves mainly in the chest region or the abdomen, sometimes the genital area and sometimes "all over".

Prepotence of the Head and the Mind in Western Culture

A Pueblo chieftain called Mountain Lake told Jung (Jung, 1963, p. 233) that his people thought all white men were mad because "they say that they think with their heads", whereas his folk thought with their hearts.

The ancient Egyptians paid scant attention to the brain, which was merely "an organ that produced mucus which came out of the nose when somebody had a cold" (Sigerist, 1951, p. 353). They evidently had little experience of "I-feeling" in the head part of their body-image.

Woodroffe (1950, p. 258) informs us "In the Indian schools the heart was considered to be the seat of the waking consciousness".

Pervading Oriental systems of medicine has been the notion of the correspondence between the human body and the cosmos. In a Vedic source quoted by Zimmer (1948, p. 115), when the Supreme Being (*atman*) commanded the life forces (*lokapala*) to enter man, fire became speech, the sun became sight, the quarters of space became hearing, the moon became breathing-out and entered the navel, and water became semen and entered the male organ.

A similar correspondence between the human body and cosmos is to be found in Chinese medicine originating in the teachings of Lao Tzu, Confucius and Mencius (Wong and Wu, 1932, p. 11). The doctrine of Yin and Yang and the doctrine of the five elements (metal, wood, earth, fire and water) both apply equally to the material universe and to the human body (the five organs), to moral and social forces, and to the configuration of the heavens.

Non-Western and pre-renaissance cosmologies tend to see the world and the universe in two kinds of ways: first, as the human body writ large (e.g. Adam Kadmon); second, as a squared circle, a series of concentric circles or of derivatives of this fourfold-circular or zodiacal synthesis. Sometimes we encounter more or less profound syntheses of these two basic schemata – the body-based schema of affect and the geometrical schema of more purely "mental" imagery (pre-thought one might term it) which Jung terms the structure of consciousness (see his "Mysterium Coniunctionis", Jung 1955/1956. See also my article on 'Things and Persons', 1982).

As far as I can tell, the only people in mankind's history who have felt the head part of the subjective body scheme to be prepotent have been the Greeks and we post-renaissance Westerners. In the opinion of Russell (1946, p. 82), the idealization of intellect began with Anaxagorus (500–428 B.C.) who differed from his predecessors in regarding mind (nous) as that which distinguishes living from dead matter. However, it was uniformly distributed in living matter and just as good in quality in animals as in man.

Both Aristotle and Plato complained that, having introduced mind as the power over all living things, Anaxagoras made very little use of it. Plato, in the Timaeus, as elsewhere, propounded a more highly differentiated view of the psyche. The irascible soul was situated in the heart, the concupiscible soul in the belly and the intellectual soul in the head. Only the last was immortal (Mettler and Mettler, 1947, p. 15).

With the re-establishment of religious rather than intellectual dominance in Western philosophy, the heart was probably once again experienced as the prepotent location of the "I". Tertullian of Carthage (155–220 A.D.) considered that the "highest faculty" of the soul was in the heart (Gordon, 1960, p. 24). Galen and the medical philosophers, however, with increasingly anatomical arguments, continued to locate the highest functions in the brain (Singer, 1959). In post-Koranic Arabian medicine, as well as in Christian mediaeval medicine, thinking was placed in the head and sensibility in the heart (Gordon, 1960, p. 118). In mediaeval thought the cosmic correspondence of the human body, at least of the Anthropos, is all-pervading; cf. the Zodiac Man of mediaeval medicine (Guthrie, 1958) and also Jung's work on Gnostic symbols of the Self (Jung, 1951).

Post-renaissance medicine has lent a spuriously crushing support for a head-dominated view of the psyche. It is completely spurious because it has confused the anatomical body with its head and brain with the subjectively felt body scheme in which, for example, what we call thinking is felt in the head, and various feelings and emotions are felt in other parts of the subjectively experienced body. The subjectively experienced body has been dismissed on "scientific" grounds because all have confused body scheme with actual body. After all, if passions are to be sought in the anatomical heart, they are hardly to be found there, even though the anatomical heart is profoundly affected by them. And so the subjectively experienced body virtually disappeared from medicine though it persisted in poetry and everyday language and has been reinstated by dynamic psychology. The Aristotelian idea that man possesses a vegetative and a sensitive soul was swept away by Descartes; he allowed but one soul, the rational one, and that was restricted to man. Its seat was in the centre of the head, the pineal gland, where mind and vital spirits intercommunicate. No doubt this was based on his actual subjective experiences, i.e. feelings and sensations seeming to originate in the middle of his head, and then rationalized and backed up by whatever scientific evidence he could lay his hands on. If I demonstrate the prepotence of the head in one's body scheme I am not proving that the subjectively experienced head is the location of the "I" feeling. However, I am of the opinion that this correlation is in fact observable. Of course not many of our predecessors were aware of the feeling of "I" being a shifting, migratory phenomenon, but would regard such migrations in concrete terms.

When I say that nowadays most Westerners, like Descartes, seem to locate their "I" in their heads, I am not claiming this is a fixed, unaltered feeling, even with those in whom it is the case (and there are many in whom it is not). The feeling of "I" is strong at some times, weak at others, and it can be distributed in differing ways in the subjective body according to emotional circumstances and according to what one is doing. One can even voluntarily shift "I" feeling from one part of the subjective body to another. For example, when I was making heavy weather walking uphill, puffing and blowing, and working the top part of my body too much, my wife said "You should walk more with your legs". By virtue of a change of conscious attitude much more of my feeling of "I" was then transferred to my legs. It was no longer a case of the "I" in my head and chest willing my legs to walk, but the "I", now in my legs, walking. With this migration of "I" feeling to where it was needed, unnecessary straining of various other parts of the body ceased. The various schools of humanistic psychology nowadays teach people to be less centred in their heads, and this again demonstrates that "I" feeling can be re-located voluntarily to a certain extent.

The feeling of "I" may be located in one part of the body-image, say the head, but it also normally has a background of positive (narcissistic) feeling from the whole of the body image. If some or most of this positive narcissistic body feeling is absent, we have a state of localized or generalized depersonalization. Depersonalization (lack of the normal background of positive "I" feeling from the whole of the body image) may spread from one part of the body to the whole of the subjective self. I am indebted to Mr Christopher Perry, who has recently given me an example of this in his patient, a young man in whom depersonalization often spread from his knees gradually to include more of his body until the whole was involved. Interestingly, this patient's first memory was of sitting in the orphanage where he spent his early years, with his knees hurting painfully from an injury.

Again, if the "I" is rigidly fixed in one place, it can be overwhelmed by excitation reaching that place (in the body scheme) from other places. I have recorded many instances in which some form of excitation "marches" (a term used to describe the spread of epileptic excitation over the body) up the subjectively experienced body until the "I" located in the head is engulfed and overwhelmed. We then have a regression-regressive behaviour, a "breakdown in defences". I argue that it cannot be a coincidence that a march of excitation until it overwhelms the seat of the "I" (wherever that happens to be located in the subjective body-world scheme) resembles so closely the march of epilepsy in the epileptic subject.

Clinical Examinations

First, however, let us examine some clinical examples of "feelings" spreading over the body and culminating in regression when they reach and overwhelm the "head" part of the body-image (when this is the locus of "I"-feeling). These case studies were mostly collected as part of a study of all the cases of depersonalization and derealization in a mental hospital over a period of two years (at least all I could find, perhaps about three dozen in all).

Case 1

The patient was a forty-year-old married woman suffering from periods of depression and of unreality and "loss of feeling". She was admitted into hospital, where episodes of acute depression, unreality and terror alternated. The following verbatim extract of an interview with me describes the almost constant battle she was at the time having to wage within herself in order to keep unpleasant, overwhelming feelings and loss of control at bay. To a large extent she could choose between sacrificing reality and "I" feeling on the one hand, and losing mental control on the other. There were two competing "I" loci at the time, one in the head and the other in the "tummy". Loss of control and regressive behaviour occurred when the excitation (quite probably sexual in fundamental nature) from the tummy reached and overwhelmed the controlling "head".

J.R. You don't seem panicky at the moment.
A.B. I'm pushing it back whatever it is. It's when things become real the panic starts. I get hysterical.
J.R. What happens?
A.B. Suppose I get interested in something. I begin to relax. Then I start to panic when I feel myself relaxed. I start trembling. Something happens in my head. I rush to a nurse and scream. They say "Pull yourself together." I do, with a mighty effort. It goes back inside. I'm back to where I started.
J.R. What happens to your head?
A.B. I don't know. I go blank. Sort of a burning sensation starts in my body and goes right over my head. I feel strange. It's happened three times in the past few days.
J.R. When it goes over your head you lose control?
A.B. Yes. I rush to the nurses screaming.
J.R. But you know what you are doing?
A.B. Yes, but I feel so strange.
J.R. How does it feel?
A.B. Sort of a feeling of nothingness except the terror that I'm going unconscious.

This patient described the spread of some sort of excitation like a fire starting in the trunk. It started when she relaxed her depersonalization/derealization defence, which she felt as an almost conscious and willed "pushing-back" of the reality and the feared feelings. The excitation rose until it reached her head, when she felt a loss of consciousness, a nothingness and regressed, rushing screaming to a nurse.

At the interview she was derealized, and described herself as feeling unreal "as if I were inside my own tummy", where everything was "twisting and burning". She also had a splitting headache. The "tummy" symptoms and the headache disappeared if she allowed herself to relax her will, when everything, including herself, became real. But the terrible price she had to pay for this was to be overcome by panic, loneliness, to allow her head to be overwhelmed by the spreading fire and to lose control over her behaviour. So she was far worse off than before. She had to re-assert her will, pull herself together and suffer the derealization, the headache and the twisting and burning feelings from her intestines.

This patient had had an operation on her abdomen in early childhood which occasioned a very painful separation from mother. This enables one to make sense of the fact that her "tummy" was unusually sensitive and seemed to be the locus of a repressed and competing "I" and source of excitation. Another way of referring to a "repressed and potentially competing 'I'" would be "complex". The locus of the complex would be a focus of excitation in the body-world schema, analogous to an epileptic focus in the nervous system (and probably having more than a merely analogic relationship).

Case 2

The patient A.B. often felt as if she were inside her own tummy, i.e. her "I" felt as if swallowed up inside herself. The next patient described a very similar set of symptoms and happenings to her "I", when excitement (this time clearly sexual) spread from her perineum to her head. (Again we must remember we are talking about the subjective body image, not the anatomical body.)

C.D. was another research patient. I saw her twice a week for several years, during which time her symptoms mostly disappeared. She was forty-five years old when I first saw her. When she was nineteen she was admitted to a mental hospital, having been found distraught, banging her head against a wall in an attempt, she said, to clear it. She was the youngest of a large family of girls all of whom bossed her. She grew up pure and childish, denied all sexual knowledge, and spent her happiest times walking in the country with a girl-friend and writing sentimental poetry. She had lived more and more in this fantasy life until her breakdown.

In childhood she had been terrified by her father and neighbour boys putting on Halloween masks and tapping on her bedroom window with a long pole with a hat on the top. In her breakdown the memories of these masks etc. turned into images of horrible, mocking faces which crowded in upon her mind. She was also tormented by "creepy feelings" "just underneath the skin" which started in the sacral region and made their way upwards to the accompaniment of great panic.

Her troubles continued in hospital. A nurse she had seen getting into bed with other female patients sat on top of her during one of her panic attacks, ostensibly to control her. She associated the nurse with her bossy sisters. An especially powerful "creepy feeling" started in her perineum and travelled up her spine toward her head. Instead of stopping before reaching the head, as had previous creepy feelings, this one, with its far greater intensity and momentum, travelled on into and around her head. She thereupon lost all self-control. She became "like a wild animal", felt "superhuman strength" (her report), threw off the nurse and after that remembered no more. She next remembered "coming to" several days later, feeling a different person. She now felt herself to be swallowed up inside her body. She felt vacant, simple-minded, childish, passively did as she was told and could not think or remember anything. In other words she avoided the sexual conflict by means of a massive regression. This episode had occurred twenty-six years before I saw her. But from that time onward she had felt herself to be inside herself and cut off from other people. Her sexual dissociation resulted in a pure and naïve manner, sentimental and poetic, and in the birth of an illegitimate child. However, she later married and had more children. There had been several spells of severe depression and anxiety during which her feeling of being cut off increased to the point of feeling as if at the bottom of a pit, tormented by horrible voices and faces and creepy creatures. During all of the twenty-six years she dreaded that the creepy feelings (which still occur, starting in the sacrum and proceeding upwards) would once again become powerful and reach her head. She imagined that if that happened she would once more become violent, only this time she would harm her children (which she had done in dreams).

One time she was sure she would be overpowered. She telephoned her general practitioner who hurried to her. He said soothing words and stroked her hair in a parental way. The creepy feelings, which had reached as far as the back of her head, retreated downwards and eventually disappeared.

Apart from the feelings of living inside herself, and of living in a pit, this patient frequently felt that her head and body did not belong to each other. Only occasionally, when she was enjoying herself dancing, did head and body join together in a harmonious whole.

Many of these feelings and feeling-states were transformed into pleasurable, opposite, feelings when, several weeks after I started to see her, she found that she had fallen in love with me (cf. Chapter 5). She was still swallowed up but instead of prison it was now a good place. The work of accepting and using her sexual feelings and her adult intellect took much longer.

Being overwhelmed, losing her "I" control, was to her being swallowed up. Even when the "I" is not intensely head-centred, loss of control is, I think, always felt as some kind of engulfment or swallowing. The word "possession" itself implies some such image, perhaps. This patient felt as if swallowed up inside herself (no doubt to protect herself from "emerging into life") for twenty-six years. All powerful feelings, including the sexual climax, were (according to her feeling) to be feared because it meant being swallowed up and also opening up and swallowing. Fear of and avoidance of commitment to others is of course a frequent concomitant of homosexual problems, when a person of opposite sex may be invested with the projection of "feared swallower".

Case 3

E.F. was a woman in her early forties who was in analysis with me over a period of six years. I saw her two and later three times a week. Her illness started several years before analysis, with spells of panic, absent-mindedness and depersonalization.

An only child, she remembered only hatred for both parents. She described her father as an aloof, impersonal disciplinarian and her mother as a timid nonentity who always sided with father. As a child she felt paralysed with fear into meekness and submissiveness when she was with her parents. When she was able to get away from them she was cheerful, often high-spirited and sometimes naughty. This cheerful "self" became her usual "self" and persisted for several years after marriage. However, her husband and mother-in-law gradually "got on top of her". She worried a great deal about her children when they came along. Finally she broke down with severe anxiety. For ten years she had had the same hatred and contempt for her husband that she had previously had for her father. Her cheerful sub-personality had been developed on the basis of a denial of her (to her bad) father's existence.

At first she was hostile and rejecting towards me, but after the first few interviews, when I concentrated in interpreting this behaviour towards me, I changed dramatically into a benign, god-like figure, able to allay her fears by merely existing. Her husband remained on the whole a somewhat hated and despised person. Anything I said which was in the least interpretable as "siding with him" or "siding with her parents" produced a calamitous state of vagueness, inertia or torpor on her part. She brought many anxiety dreams of terrifying male figures, dreams of disgusting, gruesome little faeces - animals clearly related to her children and dreams of dreadful chasms, gaps and voids, and of confusions related to separation from or misunderstandings of me.

After two years she had one of these terrifying dreams of separation from me and the appearance of the terrifying impersonal father.

> I was in your kitchen. Someone said "Come this way" and ushered me into a place like a theatre. There was a wide carpeted staircase and this person got a long way in front. Then an excited child ran in front of me and fell over and over downstairs, like a ball. I screamed to the person in front, "Don't just keep on walking. That is a child, not a ball." Then someone came to me and asked what I was waiting for. I said I was waiting to see you. The man said it was five o'clock. Five o'clock was a hideous time. My mind had gone. He said, "You'd better come out with

me". Then a dreadful man appeared with a huge stocking over his face like you wrap meat in. I went berserk. I screamed and fell back. I awoke fighting.

In our discussion of the dream she mainly talked about her fear of separation from me, which would produce the hideous distortions and transformations of the dream.

Some time later she brought the following dream:

> I was on holiday in Africa enjoying some fruit. I was with someone, looking around. Then my husband appeared and said, "Don't eat that fruit, it's poisonous". He offered me some messy, sticky cough drops, saying they would do me good. I refused, wanting something local and exciting to eat. Then I saw the local population doing a ritual penance. They all wore white and were high up on steps, each step as high as a room. They somersaulted off these steps backwards. It was a religious ceremony. If they arrived at the bottom their sins were forgiven. If not, bad luck.

She had just been on holiday with her husband, but after many quarrels she had wanted to come home. She felt as if she were on a lot of rocks, being thrown back into childhood. Everything became horrible and unreal. Her husband had treated her like a fool, she said. Everything became jumbled up.

Later she told me of a dream of being with me and another doctor. The other doctor was trying to force unpleasant medicine on her but she refused. I was neutral. She went on to talk of another woman who was always on the side of authority. I commented that this woman seemed to have had good feelings towards her parents. She said "That's right. She was always talking about her parents." There was then a silence, after which she said "I can't stand your silences. They make me think you are thinking 'I can't do anything for her'. You wouldn't say that, would you?" When I did not give her an immediate assurance, feeling rather under pressure by her, she shouted "Why don't you say something?" I said "I think we should go into all this". She immediately screamed "Say something" and somersaulted backwards over the arm of her chair on to the floor. As I helped her to her feet, I remembered the dream in which she fell backwards, and the ball/baby, and the dream of the ritual of the backward somersaults of the African tribe. I asked if I had just turned into the stocking-faced man in my refusal to reassure her. She replied "My father was very slow and pondered things. The child in that dream rolled over and over downstairs. That's just what I did." I commented that it was practically the first time she had reacted to me as if I were a bad parent. She said: "A lot of this confusion is refusal to accept that you could possibly think like that – that you would ever fail me in any way." Later in the session she remembered that the hideous time, five o'clock, of the first dream was to do with an idea she had that the analysis was to last five years, and five years only.

My wanting to talk about her fears of separation was nasty medicine to her, which she associated with the messy cough-sweets of the dream a week previously, which was followed by the backward somersaults of the religious ritual. Two weeks later there was a similar episode, except that she threw her handbag at me. She afterwards described *a feeling of power and strength that came upwards from the base of her spine and overwhelmed her head so that she lost herself.*

We have here an image of a motor impulse to scream and arch backwards in response to a delay in gratification felt as an unbearable separation in which the good parent is transformed, no doubt by her anger, into a hideously bad one. The regression might well have been to earliest infancy, a screaming when she was not presented with the nipple, and the hallucination of a hideous breast/parent, the stocking-faced (phallus) man. Here again, as the impulse takes charge, there is a sensation of the head being overwhelmed by sensations arising from below. The dream images of baby/ball and religious devotees rolling over backwards illustrate the extremely important fact that these regressive impulses and acts can be represented in imaginal form long before they are enacted, if they are enacted at all, as they were in this case because of my insensitivity.

In these three patients the regression was signalled by the overwhelming of the subjectively experienced head by impulses (wishes, sensations) subjectively arising from below and mounting upwards. An image of the head or mind being engulfed, swallowed or taken over is suggested. In some cases the person may deliberately allow his/her conscious control or detachment to be abandoned, as in the following case.

Case 4

A highly intelligent thirty-year-old engineer, after the death of his mother, felt unsatisfied with his work, and yearned for faith or for religious experience. In his search he read some books by Jung and was fascinated by the idea of the mandala. He started to paint mandalas of his own, and found that they acquired their own compelling power, of a sinister kind. He found himself painting eyes at their centre, which were also vulvas. (His father had been blind in later life.) He finally felt compelled to enter and pass through the eye at the centre of the mandala in a deliberate, ritualized act of masturbation, but he also felt that if he did this he would be lost. After an intense struggle he gave in to the compelling power of the eye and masturbated. Thereupon he became psychotic. He felt that he had lost his soul and that his heartbeats were harming his little niece in a sexual way. Therefore the only decent thing left was suicide. He took a large dose of sleeping tablets but was found some hours later by a relative who happened to call by.

Electroconvulsive therapy having failed to shake his conviction of loss of soul, he came into psychotherapy with me. During the first year, a constantly recurring theme was the image of the eye with its compelling power. He associated it with death, with the vagina and the swallowing aspects of the female, with a long tunnel and with the unknown. I encouraged him to paint and elaborate the fantasy, which resulted in increasingly complex and colourful paintings. Again he found himself drawn by the eye, and I cautiously encouraged him to proceed through it in his imagination. When he brought himself to do this, the results were very different from his first journey through the eye. This time he kept having delicious sensations. He again had ideas of magic connexions but this time of a pleasurable kind. He kept hearing music. His paintings became rather fragmented and disconnected, and contained many breasts and various objects uniting. A new phase of therapy commenced in which fantasies of breasts and buttocks were prominent.

In this patient a deliberate act of allowing his "I" to be "swallowed" was followed on the first occasion by a psychotic regression, on the second by a therapeutic one. This sort of engulfment is to be contrasted with the kind of regression of the first three cases, in which the "I" located in the mind, or the head part of the body, and not the whole "self" is swallowed up. Instead of sensations rising upwards to the head, the patient (Case 4) himself – his whole subjective self – in his imagination entered into the part of his Self represented by the eye, experienced as non-self swallower.

The second case, the woman C.D., had some of the same characteristics as the last case, as she felt herself to be "inside herself" at times, or in a pit, with auditory hallucinations of fragments of conversations and visual images of horrible faces. After a few weeks of exploration of her feelings and fantasies, she came along in a state of some excitement, saying that she felt that the only thing that would cure her was my making love to her. She felt in a pit again, but this time it was the blissful one of being "in love", from which she had no wish to escape. The horrible faces had now changed into erotic feelings and imagined kisses, the creepy feelings in her body had changed to sensations of sexual excitement. She was now having dreams in which I was chasing her and terrifying her by saying I wanted to help her.

Both Cases 2 and 4 illustrate the ambiguous nature of being "swallowed up". It may be of a psychotic nature or be more akin to a state of being in love or of religious exaltation. It may be both at the same time, at different psychic levels.

In the doctrines and practices of Kundalini Yoga, we have an example of an upward-going spread of excitation blissfully overwhelming the mind. The symbol of this excitation, this power, is the serpent, which activates each chakra or centre of existence (consciousness) as the meditating yogi allows it to arise from the lower centres.

In the Yoga of Psychic Heat, the candidate is directed to visualize the letter HAM, white of colour, inside the "median nerve" at the crown of the head, as if it were about to drop nectar. We are told:

> HAM is the Tibetan symbol for the personal pronoun 'I'. It is white, a correspondence with the sexual fluid, which its visualization sets into psychic activity . . . The HAM symbolizes the masculine aspect of the mysterious psychic fire-force; and, as a result of its union with that of the feminine aspect, symbolized by the short A, the Secret Psychic Heat is born. The Goddess Kundalini is roused from her age-long slumber to ascend to her Lord in the pericarp of the Thousand-Petalled Lotus. She first ascends, like a flame, to the Manipura-chakra, of which the navel is the hub; and the lower half of the body is filled with mystic fire. Then she continues her ascent; and in the union with her Lord, the Divine One, the whole body is filled, even to the tips of the fingers and toes, with the Secret Psychic Heat (Evans-Wentz, 1958, p. 192).

Here we have sexual images arousing sexual feelings and sensations in the lower parts of the body which rise upwards until the whole body is suffused with warmth and bliss. The most proficient adepts of this yoga are those who can melt the most snow with their naked bodies. Through their meditation and yogic practice, these adepts have learned to become consciously aware of and eventually to control the same excitations which in their negative form overwhelm our patients.

A change of auspices from those of the bad parent to those of the good parent can transform these excitations. An access of psychological insight may effect transformation, as the following case notes illustrate.

Case 5

This was a case of a woman suffering from sexual frigidity. This symptom disappeared after burning sensations spread from her head to her genital regions.

She was thirty years old when she came for treatment, having been sexually frigid since marriage seven years previously. The frigidity had become worse after the births of her two children. She had hated her father for maltreating her mother and had witnessed intercourse between them. To her, sex signified more maltreatment. These facts came to light after discussions with her general practitioner, who now suggested that she bring her husband along next time. She did so, whereupon she bickered with her husband in front of the doctor until he made her realize she was behaving with her husband as if he was her father. She went away very distressed and spent the next two days weeping, with a severe headache. She then had a crisis, as she called it, in which feelings of burning and of pins and needles spread from her head downwards into her trunk, genitals and limbs. After this her frigidity disappeared for some weeks. Later it partially returned (the therapy had not been followed up).

A psychological insight or interpretation may thus be experienced in the head as a positively charged feeling, the opposite of depersonalization, and its effect spread to other parts. In the course of my own analysis, I remember my analyst stating a "hard fact" about me which was true but unpleasant. I immediately felt a hard, painful sensation in my head. Later, on my way home, I again recalled what he had said and again felt a hard lump in my head. It felt like steel. In the course of the next few days I assimilated the fact and the sensation gradually disappeared.

Painful head feelings including headaches are often caused by other parts of the Self being denied access by the "mind". Other parts of the Self may be as it were attempting to reach the mind from below, or through the metaphorical effects of personal interaction, as in the example just given.

Case 6

A forty-year-old man, complaining of a numb, cotton-wool feeling in the head and of inability to think clearly, dreamt of an attack on a fortress by yellow men. The fortress was defended by men of the Royal Navy. In the dream he knew that the fortress was his own head.

This man had lived with his parents in British colonies until sent to school in England. His father had unmentionable local black genes in his ancestry and his mother was very white. The patient felt tainted and there was some persecution at school. The yellow men were associated with a rejected sub-personality associated with the father and the Royal Navy were associated with his untainted ideals and with his mother. The positive, longed-for aspects of his father were not apparent at the time, until homosexual wishes were analysed.

I have said enough to indicate that there is no intrinsic reason for the "I" to dwell only in the head, or for the head to dominate the total personality. However, subjective obliteration of the mind/head part of the subjective self may, in persons who normally dwell in their heads, be accompanied by marked depersonalization. Subjective engulfment may accompany regressive change; a change in behaviour.

Case 7

For a time this patient, a young woman, felt that her mind and her head had "gone". She felt for that time that she was existing in her chest.

She was an obsessional woman who suffered from periods of depersonalization and from intense fear of going out of the house. At other times she compulsively stole rubbish from dustbins and was strongly identified with rubbish herself. After two years of therapy she began to have "streaming" and "explosive" feelings in her head. These culminated in a feeling of having no head at all and of speaking from her "stomach". At the same time intimate, warm, loving, lavatory-type feelings and fantasies towards and about me occupied much of her consciousness. The stomach-location for the "I" was thus her "rubbish" sub-personality. It achieved temporary ascendancy over the head and inhibited her usual head-self and the attitudes that normally went with it.

Case 8

A similar temporary dislocation of the usual "I" from its home in the head occurred in a man of twenty-three whom I interviewed in my depersonalization research. He normally felt his "I" to be in his head. However, after a period of irksome work, voices from his chest region or his heart, one God's, the other the Devil's, started to argue as to whether he should quit. Finally the voices commanded him to cease work, and he felt compelled to obey. From that time he existed only in his chest (his head "I" having been replaced by his chest "I" presumably), governed by the voices. He knew that the "voices" were his feelings "speaking" to him, only he felt this much more strongly and literally than most people do when they say that.

After the World War II I saw several patients who had "broken down" after intense bombardment. In their role as soldiers they had been torn between duty and the wish to flee or regress. Mounting terror would culminate in a snapping feeling or some similar sensation in the head. Usually this was accompanied by a change in behaviour – screaming, cowering or running, and henceforward, until sedated, trembling and incapacitated. The snapping and breaking sensations in the head were almost invariable and were the symptom I wish to emphasize in this chapter.

The "I" as Phallus

The subject of soldiers reminds me that the "I" can be identified with the phallus. I am not speaking of the location of the "I" in the phallus (although that occurs not very infrequently) but of the image of the whole subjective self as phallus, either in its erect (phallic-narcissistic) or its limp (neurasthenic) form. The person who sees himself as the bringer-of-light often suffers from a lighthouse phallus identity.

A patient of mine had a father who was an Army sergeant-major, very upright, erect and assertive, but unfortunately more than my patient could take. He grew up timid and wilting. Usually impotent, on the rare occasions he achieved orgasm he felt his head swell to several times its normal subjective size. As his penis shrank back to its normal size, so his head shrank too.

So when the "I" is swallowed up by the "phallus" part of the body image (as in positive or negative phallic-narcissistic characters) the "head" part of the body image and the intellect may be invested with corresponding images of positive or negative excitation.

Competition between Sub-personalities

Jungian complexes and archetypes behave like personalities, and each may influence the "I" unconsciously or to varying degrees take over behaviour or "I" feeling. If I am possessed by a werewolf or vampire complex, I may be tormented by corresponding wishes or fears, or I may behave as one of these figures without being aware of it.

If we use words like "my mind", "my heart", "my soul" etc., we are often referring to sub-personalities which are very similar in nature to complexes and archetypes. Words like this have various meanings in various cultures. They cannot even be accurately translated from one language to another. They all have a long history and it is possible that they often start off in personified or quasi-personified form.

Some, perhaps all, of these sub-personalities represent, or are located, in particular parts of the body-world scheme. The Kleinian "part-objects" are obvious examples. I may become a breast-person, a phallus-person, or a container-person. I have opined in this chapter that to a large extent many of us are head-persons, although not a few are chest- or heart-persons predominantly. But as I have illustrated, if my "I" is in my head, a complex or sub-personality who lives elsewhere may set up forces which may radiate to the head. If my "head" "I" is being rigidly defended (i.e. is behaving like an encapsulated complex rather than an accessible and plastic sub-personality), my "I" may be overwhelmed by the invading excitation. It feels like being engulfed or swallowed up. Indeed it is impossible not to suspect that swallowing "mechanisms" may be involved at some neurological level.

Furthermore, competition between sub-personalities is often, perhaps always, reflected in zones or areas of tension, inhibition, or in the blocking off of radiating feelings in the body image or in the actual body, as Wilhelm Reich and his followers are continually demonstrating.

If I am a "penis-person", e.g. a phallic-narcissistic personality, there is obviously some sort of superposition at some level of penis-image and whole-body-image. Subjectively, on analysis, this comes to feel like the "I" being *swallowed up* by my "penis self" or "phallic persona", or whatever. The image of one bodily centre setting up excitation which advances on another and eventually swallows it up or interacts with it in some other rather "basic" way sounds very naïve and anthropomorphic, but this is what happens subjectively and must reflect some corresponding activity on a neurophysiological level.

Without claiming to understand the neurophysiology of all this, I feel that it is obvious that we are dealing with the spread of neuronal excitation which has features in common with the "march" of some kinds of epilepsy, and no doubt with the irradiation of "Pavlovian" excitation and inhibition.

Comparison with Epileptic Phenomena

The upward spread of polysensory excitation until it reaches the head, when self-awareness is impaired or lost, is characteristic not only of the regressions illustrated in this chapter, but also of the most commonly occurring epileptic aura.

An early description of epilepsy by Galen records how he visited a young epileptic patient who told him that his attacks "started in his lower leg and climbed upwards in a straight line through the thigh and further through the flank and side to the neck and as far as the head, but as soon as it touched the latter he was no longer able to follow" (see Temkin, 1945, p. 6). Another youth with the same onset described it as a cold breeze. Pelops, master of Galen, ascribed epilepsy to a pneumatic substance passing from the limbs into the head, causing certain forms of epileptic attack. According to Gowers (1901, p. 64), the most frequent epileptic aura is one starting in the trunk and ascending to the neck or head. When it reaches this level unconsciousness supervenes. This aura cannot be due to spread of excitation in the neocortex, but must result from excitation in rhinencephalic or subcortical centres.

It may be useful to compare an actual case of temporal lobe seizure with the cases I have described, in order to emphasize some of the important differences. Let us take the case E.G. described by Penfield and Jasper (1954, p. 27), that of a twenty year old man with a cholesteatoma just anterior to the left temporal lobe, who suffered from psychically precipitated automatism and seizures. The first attack occurred at the age of seventeen when one of his classmates at military school grabbed a rifle out of the hands of another man. He immediately had a memory of grabbing a stick out of a dog's mouth when he was thirteen. He became immersed in this recollection and was unable to speak for several seconds, after which he lost consciousness and had a convulsive seizure. The second attack occurred when a man in a night club grabbed a hat out of the hands of the hat-check girl. The third and subsequent attacks, either of automatism or proceeding to seizures, occurred after similar episodes. At operation the temporal lobe was exposed and stimulated. Stimulation at a certain point in the superior temporal convolution, and only at this point, produced an image of a man grabbing something from somebody – a stick or something. More prolonged stimulation later at the same point produced a similar hallucination followed by incoherent talk and a seizure.

In this case, as the epileptic excitation is initiated in the temporal lobe, there is an image of painful oral frustration. Or alternatively, because of the increased irritability of the region of the cortex concerned, the image of this particular type of frustration can evoke the epileptic discharge and spread.

In my Case 3, as analysis proceeded, the severity of frustration required to produced regression in the analytic situation diminished progressively until only my delay in replying was necessary to cause the regressive discharge and diminished awareness. But with this patient the dream images included images both of the frustration itself and of the response, for example both the nasty cough-sweets and the somersaulting. The dream preceding the regression contained both good and bad parents – the good and bad doctors. This episode was the first of a series of such regressions with me, after which the patient's relations with her husband improved rapidly, so that intercourse with him was once again pleasurable for the first time since the beginning of the illness. The difference is in part a difference in the ultimate accessibility to the "I" which can be achieved in successful psychotherapy. Her regression had a ritual, even a therapeutic aspect. The dreams and the behaviour at the beginning of treatment were more like Penfield's case, in the degree of automatism. For example, she would dream of being faced with a man made of stone who was utterly terrifying. She would wake from this dream to find that she had in fact been screaming in her sleep and had tried to jump out of the bedroom window, with her husband in his pyjamas hanging on to her. Such behaviour shows considerable automatism.

The similarities with epilepsy in the spread over the body and the overwhelming of consciousness allow us to wonder whether unconscious complexes involve some sort of neuronal hyper-excitability, perhaps in the rhinencephalic–centrencephalic regions. Subjectively experienced topographical spread must surely be due to topographical representation of the subjective body scheme at the pertinent neurological level. The epileptic aura may throw light on the neurophysiology of the affective body-world scheme. Kaada (1953) concludes:

> It is not unlikely that many of the complex and vague sensations occurring as aura in temporal lobe seizures may originate in these polysensory areas (amygdaloid region, hippocampus, piriform cortex, limbic area). This applies to the frequent cephalic and various types of bodily sensations preceding automatism. It should be noted that epileptic automatism is associated with lesions in the centrencephalic system as well as in the temporal lobe.

In the epilepsies, self-awareness is not lost when the functionally disorganizing epileptic neuronal excitation is limited to the cortex of the brain, but only when it spreads to the subcortical grey matter of the "centrencephalic system" (see Penfield and Jasper, 1954).

My hypothesis that the locus of an unconscious complex or other sub-personality corresponds with hyper-excitability in some sub-cortical region which has some kind of topographical bodily representation, and which may take over the normal "I"-locus, seems similar to the findings of Schilder when he says:

> Individuals in whom a partial desire is increased will feel a particular part of the body, the particular erogenic zone belonging to the desire, in the centre of their body-image. It is as if energy were amassed at these points (Schilder, 1950, p. 124).

The kind of overwhelming of the "I" which occurred in my cases seems identical with the "overwhelming excitation" associated with anxiety (originally birth trauma) and with the "ego defences" which are set up to prevent this in psychoanalytic theory (Freud, 1936). However, in this chapter I have not been dealing with the hypothetical ego or with ego-defences so much as the self-aware "I" of experience, its variable location in the body-world scheme, and with experiences of its being overwhelmed by excitation from foci in the body-world scheme outside this location.

Chapter Seven

The sub-personalities: archetypes and complexes

In psychotherapy we find that significant dream images and dream figures represent significant parts of the personality, significant sub-personalities in fact. These images usually change – evolve – during the course of a mutative experience such as analysis.

These sub-personalities can be interpreted as ways of experiencing the world or experiencing other people, but they can also be interpreted as behaviour tendencies. Let us suppose that a patient dreams of a lion threatening him or a person in his family. The lion would be (*a*) a "lion" part of himself (usually not consciously recognized as part of his repertoire of possible conscious behaviours, but nevertheless recognizable by the therapist as a behaviour tendency, e.g. the reciprocal of his timidity) and also (*b*) a way in which he tends to perceive and react to others, i.e. as if they were lions. This would only be so in certain circumstances of course. The circumstances would no doubt be elucidated by attention to the dramatic events and the other circumstances in the dream or fantasy.

If a person is usually timid, he will clearly be more likely to see other people as lions and to perceive *himself* as the one under threat. Nevertheless, we find that the lion is part of his potential behaviour, given the propitious circumstances, or that lion-like behaviour comes into prominence at some stage of his analysis.

What we refer to as the "character" of a person is therefore describable in terms of (*a*) the prominent or behaviourally dominant sub-personalities, (*b*) whether they mostly manifest themselves as behaviours or as the ways he perceives others and (*c*) how rigid and unadaptable these patterns are – how accessible to conscious awareness and choice.

If the sub-personality is deemed to have a universal human behaviour or attitude as its basis, it is referred to as an archetype. If it is deemed to have resulted from traumatic experiences (usually repeated throughout childhood) resulting in a rigid behaviour relatively split off from the conscious "I", it is referred to as a "complex". Or it may be a behaviour tendency which is simply a result of normal non-traumatic learning (introjection of positive figures for example). Such a behaviour would be relatively plastic and adaptive, and would be relatively accessible to the conscious "I". Many of the "good" figures and tendencies would come under this heading of normally plastic sub-personalities. "Internal objects" and psychoanalytic structures also come within my definition of sub-personalities.

The word sub-personality has drawbacks. One is that it would naturally be taken to convey a human quality. But sub-personalities are often "things" rather than "persons". For example, a prison (impersonal container, bad or perhaps good) could be an important sub-personality. This image would represent the patient's rigid, non-human behaviour, his rigid defensive body, his tendency to imprison his human or instinctive attributes and not let them go free. And so I propose to retain the term sub-personality even though the relevant image does not necessarily seem to be a person or to take human or even animate form.

Another drawback I have discovered in my use of the term "sub-personality" is that some people take it to mean "sub" as opposed to "super", implying "inferior" or "of lesser status". As some of the sub-personalities, e.g. some archetypes, have a divine, numinous, definitely "super" quality, a slightly "inferior" quality is definitely not intended by my use of the term "sub". I only intend to mean "partial" in the sense of "not the whole of the self or the whole person or personality". For example, if we take the Christ figure (as opposed to the historical Christ), I take this as part of the Self and not the whole Self. For example, He does not encompass the "Satanic" part or the "Virgin Mary" part of the Self. But He is super- rather than sub-human.

According to Freud (1914, p. 29), Jung's work on word association (see Jung, 1904) in the early years of this century was mainly responsible for the widespread use of the term complex. The concept of archetypal psychic structures was developed by Jung from about 1915. The concept of the complex and the concept of the archetype are possibly the two central concepts of Jung's psychopathology and psychotherapy. In general, the method of free association perfected by Freud uncovers the successive layers of the complex and the traumatic experience at earlier and earlier ages which form the core of the complex. The themes of mythology, religion and cultural activity – the psychotherapeutic activities of humans – are centred amid the archetypes, and are uncovered by the methods of active imagination and introverting activities and drugs.

The sub-personalities of the unconscious in practice are not completely divisible into these two classes. Interpretation may sometimes stress the personal, sometimes the collective aspect of a sub-personality.

Sub-personalities occur in pairs or in interacting groups. For example, a mother and infant pair, a father beating or chasing a child, a witch imprisoning and devouring a child or a pair of children, an oedipal triangle. The inter-relationships unfold according to age-old patterns and according to the personal experiences of the subject, good and bad. The conscious "I" may be in one role at one time, another at another.

Sub-personalities constitute emotionally charged underlying determinants of perception and behaviour. The conscious "I" may be cut off and defended against the sub-personality and its effects. The psychoanalysts have enumerated the various ways in which the "I" defends itself against these "shadow" aspects of the Self, but they do not emphasize the positive aspects of what is trying to come through.

The Possible Nature and Role of the Sub-personalities

Writing in 1951, Jung summarized his discoveries of archetypal motifs as follows:

> Since for years I have been observing and investigating the products of the unconscious in the widest sense of the word, namely dreams, fantasies visions, and delusions of the insane, I have not been able to avoid recognizing certain regularities, that is, *types*. There are types of *situations* and types of *figures* that repeat themselves frequently and have a corresponding meaning. I therefore apply the term "motif" to designate these repetitions. Thus there are not only typical dreams but typical motifs in the dreams. These may, as we have said, be situations or figures. Among the latter there are human figures that can be arranged under a series of archetypes, the chief of them being, according to my suggestion, the *shadow*, the *wise old man*, the *child* (including the child hero), the *mother* ["Primordial Mother" and "Earth Mother" as a supraordinate personality ("daemonic" because supraordinate)] and her counterpart the *maiden*, and lastly the *anima* in man and the *animus* in woman. . . . It is an essential characteristic of psychic figures that they are duplex or at least capable of duplication; at all events they are bipolar and oscillate between their positive and negative meanings (Jung, 1951, p. 183).

In this passage, Jung says he is using the term "archetype" to refer to human figures. However, the same archetype turns up in practice as sub-human, supra-human and "thing". For example, the mother figure can readily take the forms of spider, goddess, building or landscape, and the forms she takes are clearly derived from each other in such a way that it is clear we are dealing with one underlying figure. There may be changes during analysis, for instance in dreams, which show progressive transitions in the nature and feeling-tone of the figure, and series of dreams show these changes quite conclusively.

We usually see corresponding changes in the "father" figure during analysis, and corresponding changes in "primal scene" material, which concerns the imagery of the essential (metaphorical, affective) tone or "feel" about the interaction between the parental figures (not necessarily the actual parents) of the unconscious. In an analysis which is proceeding well, there is progressively more good feeling and creative productivity in the interaction (symbolized, for example, by a healthy child) between the parental figures, in man–woman interactions in general, and indeed in the interaction of opposites in general.

The maternal archetype merges into the archetypes of place and progress, for example the city, the utopia, the rites of passage, rebirth, and spiritual journeying ("The Archetype of the Way"). This includes caves, underground ways, forests and tunnels as well as archways and symbols of "breakthrough".

Jung was of course perfectly familiar with these non-human archetypal images. In the same essay (Jung, 1951, pp. 193–4), he described a dream in which he climbed a mountain and saw a brook, two paths leading upward, one on the left and one on the right. To the right he saw a hotel, and down below a bridge. The archetypal nature of this image was forcibly impressed upon him when he read of an allegorical journey by the sixteenth-century physician Gerard Dorn, in which the same image is described in great detail.

It is always possible to demonstrate the universal elements in any dream or experience, but we seem to have some instinctive "feel" for what is universal or archetypal, as opposed to what is more purely personal or idiosyncratic. In this sense we can say that the notion of archetypes itself has a universal, archetypal element.

That the archetypes represent, or are the result of, spontaneous psychic activity is suggested by the myth-making qualities of faulty recall or faulty memory, or the faulty transmission of messages from one person to the next. If more than twenty or thirty people are present, and hearing is made not too easy, interesting parlour games can be devised to demonstrate this myth-making element.

The experimental psychologist Bartlett (1932) used various ways of cutting down the accuracy of perception, attention and cross-checking in the laboratory subject, thus allowing what is spontaneous, wishful, archetypal to come through. The early Gestalt psychologists, using similar laboratory methods, concentrated on the ways in which we "naturally" organize perceptions, memories etc. in the absence of completely accurate perception (and obviously no perception can be completely accurate). Good Gestalten, spontaneous and expressionistic works of art, the creations of fantasy and the universal mythological themes of mankind would all therefore share a spontaneous, archetypal quality or predisposition of the psyche. Introverting (hallocinogenic) drugs and near-death states also liberate these archetypal images and experiences. Illness and childbirth and other situations of or after emotional stress share this property of enhancing the archetypal. Factual truth and psychic truth have this curiously reciprocal relationship, it seems. This is an empirical fact which makes it easy for the down-to-earth to denigrate the psychic, and for the spiritual to denigrate the material.

Dreaming is, of course, the psychic activity in which sensory input plays a relatively small part and spontaneous psychic activity a large one.

The alert, waking mind, supplied with adequate and detailed tactual input, responds accurately appropriately and in detail to the requirements of a novel situation. But we know that such conscious adaptation may involve stress, or the sacrifice of decision-making etc. The mind may restore balance or supply perspective during sleep, particularly in the dreaming times of sleep. Dreaming seems to provide an archetypically biased backlash or commentary on those daytime mental events which made most impact. The waking mental contents are assimilated, re-interpreted, dramatized, put into metaphor, reversed (e.g. subject- and object-wise), even denied, according to unconscious need.

The property of becoming unveiled when consciousness is impaired is shared by all sub-personalities – archetypes, complexes and thoroughly learned behaviour. All of these share a tendency to be acted out in the behaviour of the person who is at a particular time or as a general rule without awareness or conscious imagery. Only when partially blocked do these sub-personalities give rise to "mental" content. There is a reciprocal relationship between acting-out on the one hand and richness and intensity of conscious experience on the other. Jung, in the same vein, spoke of a polarity between the instinctual and spiritual aspects of the archetype.

These abstract generalizations about the interaction between outer truth and inner truth, day-time and night-time psychic activity, between conscious and unconscious, had better be illustrated by one or two stories which are quite true but so commonplace as to enable it not to matter too much whether true or invented.

We are all, I think, familiar with the fact that after a hard day's driving we tend to be driving all night, in and out of restless sleep. For a week or two after my annual sailing holiday most of my dreams are about sailing. The particular contents nevertheless reflect one's underlying complexes and conflicts. And gradually the maritime world is replaced by the usual dreaming world as the dream-tide carries us inexorably homewards. But the best example of the dream providing the archetypal commentary on the day's activity comes from a mountaineering episode when I nearly perished apparently owing to recklessness but in reality due to unconscious regressive fantasies or wishes to merge with the Great Mother – a common form of "death wish".

As a seriously over-worked doctor in a mental hospital, I desperately felt the need to get away to the hills for a weekend, on my own. It was wintertime and I was walking and scrambling up a mountain in Scotland. I was making my way up the side of a steep gully made by a mountain torrent far below. The sides of the gully became steeper and more icy as I progressed upwards, but I stubbornly kept on until I slipped. Luckily I did not fall far, but instead frightened myself sufficiently to bring me to my senses and persuade me to retrace my path and proceed upwards by a gentler route. I was a little shocked by my foolishness but nevertheless had a most enjoyable and exhilarating day. After an evening of drinking and talking by a smoky fire, I settled down in my hotel bedroom. As I approached sleep my mind kept on returning, with a panicky start of my whole body, to the moment of losing my foothold. In the dream I plunged into the dizzy darkness of the deep cleft. After several repetitions of the panic, the image turned to one of wonder. The mountain was now a great mother-goddess, the gully the cleft between her legs, my plunge a blissful union succeeded by flights of exploration in the caverns inside the mountain-mother. Soon I fell into a deeper, refreshing sleep, full of wonder and pleased with these insights into my foolhardiness and my need to get away to the mountains.

My wonder and gratitude for the whole real-and-dream-experience persist. But apart from these feelings which are sufficient in themselves, I had better enumerate in more detail the role of the dreaming, archetypal experience of the "incestuous" image.

(1) It played a vital part in the acquisition of climbing skill, in which recklessness/panic is replaced by care and enjoyment.

(2) (In other words) It enabled complex-driven activity to be replaced (to a certain extent) by ego-integrated activity. The complex-driven need to seek the hills and perish in them was replaced by enjoyable and wondrous feelings about the mountains and awareness of actual dangers. Choicelessness was replaced by choice.

(3) The dream experience, pursued to its resolution, enabled me to sleep deeply and restfully. Failure to reach this core or resolution would be reflected in continued restlessness and fearful imagery.

(4) It enabled me to avoid becoming "stuck" on mountaineering or (and?) developing a phobia of it (not a small benefit).

(5) The image enabled me to relate the narrower everyday aspects of climbing with my primordial imagery, hence to my deeper, inner self. Poetic imagery always has this function, not merely for oneself but for others. I do not claim that my account has any poetic quality, although the incestuous image is a universal one. My purposes are merely expository, thus eschewing any vital aspirations which the theme warrants.

The relating of the daytime activity to its psychic roots is in my view of the essence of archetypal experience. Unfortunately for the simplicists, it need not be conscious. My "daring" to have the incestuous image was of course important, an important integrative attribute which can be learned (e.g. sometimes taken in from an analyst). However, in my opinion, a person who was unable to have such an image consciously might still escape the neurotic, complex-driven impasse because some such beneficial dream activity would occur entirely unconsciously. The distinction between normal integrative learning-from-experience and neurotic fixation would lie much more in the actual archetypes involved than in the degree of awareness. If the terrifying Great Mother has not been "worked through" to Her basic ambivalent or positive aspects, no daytime experience of this sort would be valuable, i.e. integrable. What, in turn, does this depend on? It depends in practice on the sufficient experience of love, goodness or non-disaster in situations (i.e. relationships) in life when the Great Mother was being most powerfully constellated (i.e. when one is in a very "regressed" or "in love" state). Naturally the earlier experiences are the most formative. By the constellation of an archetype or complex we mean the coming-to-life of the said sub-personality in a relationship or psychic situation. Some of the skill of the Jungian analyst consists of developing an awareness of the atmosphere of the relationship at any one time and relating it to the unconscious contents in play. There is nothing mysterious about this. The figures in question occur in the cultural history, family history, the life history, the dreams and the behaviour of the analysand, so their presence in the here-and-now of the actual situation of the moment is not surprising if one can see the wood as a whole as well as the trees. One is using oneself and one's feelings and reactions as an instrument for observing the archetypal forces in play.

Spirit and Instinct

My second story concerns more the relationship (the reciprocal one, on the whole) between the "acting-out" of a sub-personality and the experience of it in awareness. Jung referred to the archetype as having two poles, namely, the spiritual pole and the instinctual one (i.e. to do with the relatively unconscious acting-out of behaviour tendencies or behaviour patterns). I refer to a principle of reciprocity between I-possession and behavioural-possession by sub-personalities.

Most of our motor actions are carried out unconsciously or fairly unconsciously. For example, much of our driving on the road and our movements about the house, opening and closing doors etc., is performed in a fairly automatic way. Only special, unaccustomed or difficult elements are sure to enter our consciousness; this is of course a tremendously complex subject and the only point I am making here is that many habitual acts are not very conscious. The same applies to the acting-out of "instinctual" patterns and to the behaviour determined by unconscious complexes. The pattern tends to become more conscious when acting-out is blocked or partly prevented. This simple fact seems to me to underlie the tendency of archetypes to polarize into instinctive behaviours at one extreme and spiritual or numinous experiences at the other, when subjective experience is maximal and instinctive action minimal.

Many destructive actions, for example violent crimes including murder, seem in general to be carried out in a state of diminished awareness. When the person is possessed by a violent sub-personality, acting-out may occur in a fugue state or in a state of which he says afterwards "I don't know what came over me".

In his essay "On psychic energy", Jung (1928) opposes the instincts and individuation, and says

> Over against the polymorphism of the primitive's instinctual nature there stands the regulating principle of individuation. Multiplicity and inner division are opposed by an integrative unity whose power is as great as that of the instincts. Together they form a pair of opposites necessary for self-regulation, often spoken of as nature and spirit. These conceptions are rooted in psychic conditions between which human consciousness fluctuates like the pointer on the scales (Jung, 1928, p. 51).

It is clear from the context that Jung is taking a position in opposition to what he takes to be Freud's standpoint. He goes on: "Thus every child is born with an immense split in his make-up" (ibid., p. 51). He is here referring to an opposition between unmitigated sensuality and a highly differentiated spiritual inheritance. Earlier in this essay he describes how instincts may come to be canalized or transformed for socially useful purposes, citing the Wachandi of Australia (ibid., p. 42). Every spring they dig a hole shaped like a vulva, set it about with bushes, dance around it, holding their spears like erect penises, then thrust in their spears. Thus sexual libido is transformed into energy for agriculture by means of the dance, in Jung's view.

Jung was of the opinion that when the libido's outward flow is blocked, it flows internally, activating the "primordial images". This accords with what I have just said about the reciprocal relationship between "acting-out" and conscious awareness. Similarly, in his essay "Psychological factors determining human behaviour", Jung (1937, p. 114) gives a condensed outline of his conception of instincts, archetypes, modalities of psychic functioning and complexes. He describes instincts as structures essentially *outside* the psyche which have a compulsive nature, whereas what we *experience*, and what is determining, is the corresponding structure *inside* the psyche, the psychized aspect of the instinct as it were.

In this essay he lists five instincts, namely hunger, sexuality, the drive to activity, the reflective instinct and the creative instinct. To this list of instincts he adds a list of modalities of psychic functioning, including the conscious versus the unconscious, extraversion versus introversion, and the one of special interest here, namely upward versus downward, spirit versus matter.

I shall return to the dichotomy between spirit and matter later in this chapter, and to the winning of consciousness and choice in Chapter 8. In this essay Jung attributes the formation of complexes to this splitting tendency of the psyche. Complexes, like archetypes, behave like independent beings, but are specifically related to instincts in so far as instincts which have undergone too much psychization can take their revenge in the form of complexes (Jung, 1937, p. 123).

In order to describe realistically the sort of relationship we encounter in analysis between the acting-out of what may be instinctual or in some cases habitual behaviour tendencies, on the one hand, and archetypal imagery on the other, I shall describe the case of a young woman whose marriage was in some difficulties. She was devoted to her children and had strong religious beliefs. She became strongly attracted to another man but one day, after a long talk with him, she decided not to embark upon a physical relationship. That night she dreamt of a dragon-like monster which was trying to break into her house. She saw the dragon's claws scattered on her pillow, and on waking immediately recognized them as the bitten finger-nails of her childhood. In this vein she realized that the dragon represented her childish lust or greed which was threatening her home. Furthermore, she recognized certain devouring tendencies which she had as a mother which when thwarted might often give place to furious smashing-up feelings towards the children.

When we speak of her strong wish to "act out" her sexual attraction, her anger with husband and family and her greedy, deprived feelings, we are making a clinical appraisal of the kinds of "instincts" with which we find we have to deal in analysis as well as in everyday life. This formulation would have a multitude of other clinical observations to support it.

The "primordial image" of the dragon – how much more primordial could one get than a dragon? – which I say was activated by the conflict over the would-be lover, referred more to her own blocked "instincts" than to the apparent object of her desire. The dragon clearly represented the angry, deprived child in her as well as the destructive devouring mother. But we know that the devouring mother we encounter so often in casework *is* the deprived child in the mother concerned, so there is only one figure here, not a double meaning. And so it was the manner and the meaning of the blocked-off love-making which gave rise to the archetypal dream image, as well as the tremendous power of her attraction.

Again it is clear that conflict-free, instinctual or habitual activity does not give rise to archetypal activity, but that it is the unintegrated parts of the Self which when activated and blocked give rise to archetypal activity and to the potentiality for conscious integration – the images in other words convey the "meaning" of the blocked-off bits of the Self. These are the emergent parts of the personality, the growing points of the developing person.

Mind and Matter

If "spirit" is higher than "instinct", then lower still we have "matter". Is there really a continuum of this sort? I mean in fact. If so we have to revise our physics.

Like projection, acting-out can be regarded as a way of discharging otherwise unbearable psychic contents. We are referring to bits of the Self which have it seems to be exteriorized.

It is very disturbing to be confronted by the schizophrenic patient who feels he has to commit murder to relieve some unbearable headache or tension within himself. Sometimes the act happens and the relief is obtained. The relief afforded by projecting bad parts of the Self on to others is surely familiar to all of us. Then we have, I believe, the conversion of bad feelings into actual material outer phenomena like poltergeists and "psychic" phenomena. When we talk about split-off parts of the Self we may be talking about physical energy, even material objects. So is psychological splitting, the abandonment or non-attainment of responsibility for parts of one's Self, the same thing as materialization, the conversion of mind into matter? Let us stay with this idea.

These "materializations" are felt in the air, in the emotional atmosphere, the "vibrations" that tell us what sub-personality is being activated. When the emotional atmosphere between Freud and Jung was becoming so highly charged (Jung, 1963, p. 178) that it was beginning to be no longer possible for them to be together, there was some such split. Jung felt red-hot sensations in his diaphragm which culminated in a loud report from the bookcase nearby. At this time both men were hardly able to speak to each other, and the enmity could presumably only be borne by Jung when split off in this way. Jung was a mediumistic person in whom such physical manifestations were not unknown, as his autobiography testifies.

Mary Williams, in her paper "The poltergeist man" (Williams, 1963), describes a patient who was surrounded by poltergeist phenomena which subsided during psychotherapy. They behaved like split-off complexes or unconscious contents which could be interpreted as if they were dream material or any other unconscious content. It was the degree and intensity of the splitting process which determined the degree of "materialization".

Thus it seems that it is not so much the nature of the complex which becomes split off in this way (as physical energy or matter) – violence and incestuous impulses are not unknown as unconscious forces in all of us – but the violence of the repudiation or abnegation itself which seems to distinguish between the integration of shadow contents at one extreme and the conversion into matter at the other.

Jung's concepts of the psychoid, and of synchronicity, concern the same phenomena. Jung's "psychoid" is the area between the merely vitalistic functions of living creatures and of the nervous system, on the one hand, and the properly psychic on the other (Jung, 1958, p. 176). Archetypes are psychoid in nature (ibid., p. 435). Synchronistic phenomena cause us to ascribe to the moving body "a certain psychoid property" which, like space, time and causality, forms a criterion of its behaviour. These phenomena mean that we must completely give up the idea of the psyche being somehow connected with the brain (ibid., p. 505).

Synchronicity postulates an irrepresentable element of meaning in our picture of the world, just as the introduction of time as the fourth dimension in modern physics leads us to postulate as irrepresentable the space–time continuum. The advantage of introducing the postulate of synchronicity is that it makes possible a view which includes the psychoid factor in our description of nature, that is, an *a priori* meaning or "equivalence" (ibid., p. 513).

Williams (1963) states Jung's conclusions even more boldly and says that the psychoid area "lifts the embargo imposed by cause-and-effect thinking and brings us to the point when the image and its concrete representation are one".

My own related hypothesis is that the relationship between psyche and matter is that the latter arises out of some sort of psychic splitting and is more to do with the denial or suppression of meaning than its acknowlegement. In other words, "synchronicity" is meaning breaking through, and matter is meaning split off from psyche.

Let us suppose that an inventor with unbearable anal-erotic tensions can obtain relief by inventing a machine which expresses these tensions. The invention takes on an existence of its own, and thus split-off complexes can act as material objects *in practice* (apart from abstruse theories about the relationship between Mind and Matter). Something like this may have happened in the invention of the jet engine. To understand and control this machine requires more humans to split themselves apart in a way similar to the split in the inventor. And so from a practical point of view what I am saying about the relationship between "mind" and "matter" is self-evident. Only the theory of the relationship between the two has not yet been worked out.

It is strong emotions that are generally associated with archetypal images and archetypal experiences, with complexes and, in all probability, with paranormal psychic phenomena and with extra sensory perception. But quite often these strong emotions are to some degree split-off from the normal "I" of the subject concerned. I am suggesting here that such parts of the self can be split off to the point of taking on material existence, and that the essential relationship between psyche and matter is of this nature. Sub-personalities, matter and energy may all be the same thing.

According to this hypothesis, we have spiritual or aware experience at one end of a continuum, "acting-out" halfway along, and pure matter at the other end of the continuum. Matter would then represent an extreme degree of split-offness or alienation. The continuum is well established, I believe, as far as "awareness" and "acting-out" are concerned, but the extension of the same idea to poltergeists, paranormal phenomena and to the ultimate nature of matter is of course speculative, except from a purely practical aspect.

Chapter Eight

The winning of conscious choice: the emergence of symbolic activity

In this chapter I hope to describe how unconsciousness (unconscious acting-out, unconscious identifications) can be given up and thereby replaced by conscious awareness and choice. I shall explain how "symbols" emerge into consciousness as part of this change. What I mean by these various terms will become clear as I go along, I hope. In other words, this chapter is about how sub-personalities become more integrated with the whole personality. I regard this process as the one which underlies therapy and the one which constitutes the only hope for present-day civilization.

For example, I shall describe how a little boy was able to stop behaving in a restless, aggressive, unsatisfiable way, and how a "lion" symbol emerged at the same time in his play with the therapist. In other words, "lion-like" behaviour gave place to a "lion" symbol, and at the same time he became able to choose whether or not to "be a lion".

This change is necessary before we can speak meaningfully of responsibility or of a responsible attitude towards one's own behaviour. It is of the utmost importance for politicians, lawyers and those concerned with education to understand thoroughly the facts about responsibility and the ability to use symbols and exert conscious choice. As much or most of our corporate and political behaviour is of the pre-responsible, choiceless sort, it seems vital for the future of mankind to take these facts to heart, rather than as at present functioning on choiceless unconscious acting-out and on the use of moralistic platitudes and concretized, externalized self-symbols such as the group, the nation, the ideal society etc.

In his "Alchemical studies", (Jung, 1957) Jung (p. 45) says that his chief aim in therapy is to labour with the patient towards the detachment of consciousness from the object, towards the dissolution of "participation mystique", whereby unconscious contents are projected into the object, in a state of unconscious identification. When Freud said "Where id was, there shall ego be", he was saying the same sort of thing in his own terminology. They are voicing the hope of culture and civilization in the face of blind instinct, but they both know that the hope depends paradoxically in giving full value to instinct and the unconscious, and not in the one-sided (and therefore blind) worship of ideals and idols. And both Freud and Jung were good clinicians who on the whole knew when it was wisest to let the dragon slumber in its lair, and when not to go disturbing forces in the face of whose power they were themselves impotent.

A symbol has to be defined in terms of the use that can be made of an image, act etc. by the person or persons concerned, rather than in terms of the image or act itself. Thus defined, the symbol is at the growing point of therapy or personal development. Symbols arise when an individual is preparing to give up a bit of unconsciousness, or, conversely, when the unconscious is preparing to yield up one of its treasures.

Whether or not the "I" can gather, work on and eventually enrich itself from this world of potential value which we now tend to call the unconscious depends on the working relationship between "I" and the unconscious, a talent, a gift and a skill which can be learned and which is the most priceless thing in life. Jungians often refer to it as the ego–Self relationship. [For an introduction to the topic the reader is referred to Jung (1945) *Coll. Wks* 7, "The relation between ego and unconscious".] The ego–Self relationship is essentially an "I–Thou" relationship and is at the basis not only of the relationship between "I" and unconscious, "I" and God, "I" and one's potential creativity, but also at the basis of deep personal relationships, starting with, and being greatly dependent upon, the first relationship with the mother (see for example Newton and Redfearn, 1977). When this relationship is destructive or uncreative, work on the relationship between the partners in the analysis is often necessary in order to lay the foundation of a more satisfactory I–Self relationship.

The difficulties and obstacles we have in benefitting from unconscious products are themselves largely unconscious. These difficulties are of the same general sort as those we have in relating creatively to other people. As I have said, the prototype and the environmental factor at the roots of the ego–Self relationship, including these difficulties, is the infant's relationship with his/her mother – or, at least, the relationship with the mother as remembered, reconstructed and fantasied by the analysand, which is a somewhat different thing, of course. This assertion seems to me to be supported by the following empirical fact. We find that the analyst's holding, validating and reflective behaviour towards the analysand can eventually be introjected (learned, copied at a deep level) by the analysand and thus modify or transform his ego–Self relationship. This suggests very strongly that the infant introjects his mother's holding, validating and reflective behaviours and that these latter form an important part of what we call the ego and/or the self, and even of those integrating and harmonizing functions associated with the Jungian Self. The mother reflects upon and reflects back the child's communication and behaviour, allowing the child essential space in which to act and experiment, and thus lay the foundations for the "I"–Self relationship and the ability to play and to use symbols.

In therapy (hopefully less and less as therapy proceeds) the therapist may have to mediate for the analysand this symbolic capacity, this "transcendent function" between conscious and unconscious. Dependence in the relationship between patient and therapist, Jung said, (Jung, 1916) can be seen as a measure of the degree to which the patient is lacking in his ability to relate his consciousness with his unconscious (Jung, 1916, p. 74); combined, I should add, with the degree to which he, the patient, is able to use the therapist to compensate for this lack.

Jung considered that the consciousness of children, primitive man, neurotic and psychotic persons are relatively weak and permeable. The barrier function of consciousness may be lacking altogether. There is a localized or general lack or deficiency of the "as if" attitude of consciousness towards the unconscious contents. Thus the Cameroons witch-doctor wearing the lion mask is not just pretending to be a lion, he *is* a lion (Jung, 1964, p. 44). Similarly, for a schizophrenic patient of mine, when I prevented her from rushing out into the street, I was not just *like* the Devil, I *was* the Devil (or so she said in a way which I experienced as literal and very chilling). The same may apply to the young child, and to the neurotic person in certain areas.

As the consciousness of the child, in this sense, is relatively undeveloped, and the symbolic function likewise in a rudimentary state, it is in children, and in our child analysands in particular, that we may most readily and simply observe the development of the symbolic capability, the emergence of symbols, and the way symbols are used.

The function of holding-together or containing opposing or conflicting wishes is itself often symbolized by a container or circumscribed area. For Jung, the alchemical vessel in alchemy, the protected part of the Self where transformative experiences can be rehearsed and resolved symbolically, represents an important development in the consciousness of mankind. The temple, the walled city, the stage of the theatre and the frame of the picture are all examples of the same thing.

This containing capacity, at first mediated by the mother, is experienced and hopefully finally introjected by the child and becomes the child's ability to contain his impulses and conflicts to the extent that usable images and symbols arise in consciousness. Urinary and other sorts of continence may be an important bodily expression of progress in this holding capacity. But what does this holding and containing mean in parental and therapeutic practice?

Some of the clearest and simplest examples of the process of symbol formation, showing the various factors involved, are provided by child analysts (e.g. Fordham, 1969, chapter 10). Let me quote from a paper by Dorothy Davidson (1979, pp. 36–7), a London child analyst showing how the analyst's "holding" behaviour enabled restless, aggressive, hungry and unsatisfied (lion-like) behaviour in a four-year-old child to be given up and replaced by concern for the analyst with the concomitant emergence of a "lion" symbol. In my terminology the "lion" is here an oral, sadistic complex which shows itself in behavioural terms but which with therapy comes to be experienced as or represented by a lion symbol and related with the "I" of the child. John was a very disturbed and restless child of four when he started analysis with Mrs Davidson. There was

> a search for something . . . someone to contain him. He tried various chairs and a couch but could only remain on them for a few moments. Then he would hurl himself off or out of the chair, creating the impression of having been thrown out. This theme culminated in the following way. John made what he called a cage for himself out of some furniture. He now spent the great part of his sessions inside his cage and said he was a lion. From time to time he would rush out of his cage and attack me, but then there was a change; prior to it he had really attacked but now he was *pretending* to scratch and bite me. These attacks seemed to belong to his oral impulses and phantasies represented in the image of a lion who came out for a feed. One day, John, sitting in his cage as usual, said: 'The lion is hungry – don't let him out.' There was a new note in his voice and an expression in his eyes which I had not seen before, and I recognized it as concern. He had been able to put his dilemma into words. I responded to this by saying that I knew the lion was hungry and needed to come out and eat me – but that he, John, loved me and did not want to eat me up. He smiled and said 'Feed him in his cage'. Accordingly I gave him pieces of plasticine, which he pretended to eat. At the same time I talked to him about having been held in his mother's arms and being fed by her. He replied 'Like this'. After another feed John enlarged the cage; then he announced 'The lion wants to come out – he needs a lead'. I tied some string to John's buttonhole at his request, then he said, 'He needs a label' and asked me to write on it 'John Lion'. He now came out of his cage with me holding the string. When the session ended he went off holding my end of the string and said he was leading his lion home. Only later did I discover that he had also taken a small police car! This seemed to symbolize his growing ability to manage the affects represented by the lion.

The next day John made Mrs Davidson pretend to be a witch who could turn him into a lion, but this was all right if he could hold on to a "John" label. From this play Mrs Davidson understood that John was searching as if for a feeding breast and also for containment, and that, through finding these at least in a token way within the transference relationship with her, he was able to enact the fears, fantasies and destructive impulses which up till then had overwhelmed him.

Of course there are a lot of questions, left unanswered here, regarding what constitutes an effective token satisfaction. How non-concrete or non-literal can or must it be in order to push forward the therapy? The answer, rather maddeningly I am afraid, depends on the stage of development of the consciousness of the child or patient. Parents and therapists develop a fairly unerring "feel" for this.

This account of six weeks play therapy conveys the relatively complex, skilled and sensitive talk and behaviour subsumed under the simplistic heading of "the analyst's containing function", or "the analyst's holding behaviour" etc. I should like to emphasize a few of the features which seem to be important in this "holding".

(1) A warm, caring relationship had been established. It is implicit in John's concern for the analyst.
(2) The analytical setting, and Mrs Davidson's friendly tolerance, gradually resulted in the "cage" play. The cage having been established – an additional safety boundary within the therapy room – the hungry lion can now be enacted in play and the oral aspects of the restless behaviour and dissatisfaction worked on.
(3) Mrs Davidson's own play responses were sufficiently concordant with John's feelings and play as to enable John to go forward in his play. Thus she did not give oral interpretations until these were initiated by John's intimation that the lion was hungry. Even this short extract contains many examples of how she was able to meet and gently push forward the play and hence the therapeutic process.
(4) The restless, aggressive behaviour – the lion behaviour – is "tamed" by Mrs Davidson's fortitude (in coping with the real attacks), therapeutic skill and the warmth and security of the therapeutic relationship and setting. John's concern for the therapist then enables him to do his own containing (caging), a benevolent caging learned directly from her behaviour towards the restless lion. This degree of concern may of course not be there and may take a long time to develop, but it may be an essential stage in the replacement of acting-out behaviour by symbolic activity.
(5) Mrs Davidson's interpretation of a "lion" part and a "John" part was intended to help John to differentiate out and at the same time contain two opposing sub-personalities in his Self. The ability to differentiate out and contain opposing tendencies and wishes is often referred to by analysts as the ego function of "containing ambivalence" or "containing the opposites". No choice is possible until containment ("continence") is achieved, i.e. until Mrs Davidson's containing behaviour has been taken aboard by John.

(6) The lion's lead, the link between the tamer and the lion – later the tamer is John himself, John's ego – is worth noting. String and other symbolic links are often of vital importance in the process of symbol formation. Once the container is securely internalized, the external string can be relinquished and the internal link between the ego and the symbolic activity is sufficient. Mrs Anne Brown, a child analyst trained at the Society of Analytical Psychology in London and now working in Australia, told me of a case of hers (personal communication) of a four-year-old child who at the beginning of therapy was virtually mute. His play at first largely consisted of the use of string in linking with Mrs Brown and binding them together. As the relationship was established, the string play was relinquished and replaced by other forms of play, and talking was now possible. In therapy token links are often necessary in the transition period in which the therapist's mediation and containing function is being gradually internalized and taken over by the patient.

(7) The confusion of and about John's initial behaviour was gradually clarified as John was helped to distinguish and separate out the "lion" part of himself that wanted to burst forth and eat up the analyst (which emerged more clearly as it was caged and became a "pretend" part) and the John part who was responsible and who cared for the analyst. In other words, the symbol only emerges clearly out of the unconscious matrix of acting-out once the "as-if" aspect is clearly established. The "as-if" aspect ("I am only *pretending* to kill you, eat you, be dead, etc.") enables play to go forward and the symbolic image to develop fully. If this essential boundary of the awareness of metaphor is not yet established, the individual *behaves* as if the metaphor were a fact. For example, John might be acting out the lion and hallucinating the witch. But of that we can never *be* sure, as the metaphor – in-action, the "unconscious fantasy" – can only be inferred from the behaviour, including the verbal behaviour.

It would be unwise to advance this observation to the status of a general hypothesis. For example, clear images may emerge into consciousness before the corresponding behaviour is anywhere near to being able to be given up or not be given up as a matter of choice. There is often a splitting between image and corresponding affect which is used defensively (intellectually, for instance) in order to delay affective (moral) responsibility and autonomy.

There may of course be various reasons for not acting out our impulses, e.g. fear as well as love. But it seems to me that impulses inhibited because of fear become incorporated into the shadow along with the hated part of the person responsible for the fear, whereas impulses inhibited because of concern become a part of the self available to the normal adaptive "I" and are "I"-enhancing. It goes without saying that choiceless behaviour (the unintegrated "sub-personality") can be "given up" for the sake of persons other than the mother or analyst, and for the sake of idealized or loved internal objects and abstract principles, such as democracy and liberty, and for the sake of ethical considerations.

So much for the emergence of symbol and conscious choice in a child. The achievement of "consciousness" in the sense in which I have used the term consciousness is always a relative affair. One could never be "completely conscious" of a lion sub-personality, any more than one could be in complete charge or in complete rapport with a lion. A certain amount of wisdom, a certain amount of courage, a certain give-and-take will help enormously, but the relationship between oneself and one's lion is never settled once and for all.

The taming of the lion may become a habitual act and in this sense the lion will go back into the unconscious. Only when restlessness or appetite are stimulated (by fatigue, hormonal changes, dissatisfactions and frustrations) may the lion then be awakened and become a problem. Much of our everyday behaviour is unconscious in this sense of being habitual. I do not believe there is any essential (neurophysiological) distinction between the unconsciousness of the way we walk about and open and close doors and go upstairs or downstairs without counting the steps, and the unconsciousness of John's lion-like behaviour before the lion symbol emerged. The symbolic activity (consciousness of the sub-personality in question) only arises when necessary, when the unconscious activity is called into question for one reason or another.

Of course repression and other "defences" are very real phenomena. They reflect negative feelings between sub-personalities, for example between the present "I" and a given sub-personality. The negative relationship can be of many different kinds and the concept of repression is too general to be of much use in therapy at our present more sophisticated stage of development.

In therapeutic work, symbols do not arise in the patient so much as in the interaction between patient and therapist. They do not emerge out of the patient's unconscious into the patient's consciousness, but they arise out of a shared unconscious into a shared consciousness, so to speak. Shared consciousness and shared responsibility is often how progress comes about.

To illustrate this I should like to describe the emergence of a symbol in the relationship between one of my analysands and myself. There is absolutely nothing remarkable about it. Its everyday nature gives a fairer idea of the work of analysis than the occurrence of a shattering experience or revelation, although these latter certainly occur. The "symbol" was of a rapist/robber who later developed into an ant-like creature who was trying to break down a barrier and reach a treasure.

For my own convenience, I asked my patient if he could come an hour later each week for his Friday morning session. He raised many objections and the atmosphere between us became very tense. I felt I had to say that I was not going to make an issue of it but it seemed necessary to discuss our feelings about it. It emerged that he was experiencing me as a robber/violator in asking for the change in times. In fact, any demand on him to change himself or his arrangements etc. was experienced by him thus. On my part, I was experiencing him as a somewhat selfish person incapable of considering other people's needs or of "putting himself out" for anyone else. When we were able to get some sort of picture of the robber/rapist which had pervaded the emotional atmosphere between us, we had arrived at a useful symbol, symbolic both for him and for me, which we often later used in our analytic work. We were able to compromise on the matter of times of sessions. We were able to go on and relate the robber image with aspects of his father. The robber was also prominent in the mutual projections between the parents and in the rows between them over money etc. He was also present in the victim/persecutor relationships affecting his family throughout the generations.

A few weeks later he dreamt of trying to go to a Jungian seminar given by an elderly friend who actually gives such seminars. His somewhat free associations with this friend included references to his friend's bedroom in which were photographs of her late husband, and comments on the friend's large double bed. In the dream my patient could not get to the seminar but ended up in a cul-de-sac called Anterix Road. His associations with this word Anterix were with the vagina seen as a forecourt to the cervix and womb. He could reach the forecourt but could not penetrate into the womb, the inner place where the source of value and rebirth lay, which was also the parents' bedroom. So he associated this dream with feeling kept out of what is of most value in life.

The next day he came to the session saying that he felt agitated and felt like screaming. I invited him to look into this feeling. He said he imagined himself as an ant with long antennae trying to get through a thick wall. On the other side of the wall there were red and green jewels shining, and a white light was present in their vicinity. He was able to identify the ant with the rapist/robber, and the wall with his own defences against the rapist/robber in himself. The ant of course represents that which, when projected, his defences are trying to keep out. When his feeling of "I" is inside the wall or temenos he has a feeling of self but often feels insecure and projects the robber on to his environment. When his "I" is outside the wall, he has no feeling of self and is a mass of sensations and murderous impulses, possessed by envy.

The image of jewels and light surrounded by a relatively impenetrable defence is of course like a mandala. Let us digress in order to clarify the meaning of this symbol. As I have just indicated, the meaning of such a symbol depends very much on where the "I" is located relative to it. If the "I" is identified with the treasure or with the mandala as a whole, it means a "self" which hopes for continence and security. The wall or barrier surrounding the contents serves to defend this "self" from outside threats and to stop harmful contents and treasured contents from getting out. The thickness of the wall therefore is a measure of insecurity, and the mandala is an ideal, a wish in the face of an insecurity due to his own needy, excluded feelings which constitute the strength and subjectively felt danger of being invaded, broached and plundered. When his "I" is located in the ant/robber, the treasure inside the barrier is experienced as unattainable, and is in fact unattainable because of the strength of his own defences against his robber sub-personality. How this insecurity came about, how the defences had to be erected against invasive (needy) parents, is another story.

These thick barriers in the personality constitute important blocks against freedom and happiness. We have a situation of envy, in which what is on the other side of the barrier is idealized and unattainable and subject to envious, destructive attacks.

If I and my treasure are constantly under threat from the robbing invader, I may try to make my house beautiful and am always finding things wrong that have to be attended to. I may always be worrying about my financial security and my professional status in the face of envious colleagues, and I may always be worrying about pains and other hypochondriacal threats. These fixed aims and attempts to concretize the mandala motivate my life long before the mandala is constellated. Only when the mandala is constellated and really reflected upon can security become a possibility because it can now be given up. The attainment of the treasure is now a possibility because the ant no longer has to be kept out. In other words, one can now give up one's paranoid defences. Of course not everyone who dreams of mandalas or paints them does give up his paranoid, envious sub-personalities. But with help or therapy it would be more likely to happen.

In the mental sphere, a feeling of stupidity, thickness, inability to get at the desired knowledge or take things in may result from the same barrier in oneself.

After this work my patient was more able to empathize with others. This represented an increased ability for his "I" to cross the self/not-self barrier, now much less impenetrable.

The treasure or the transformation inside the container represents *both* the ultimate regression (to the "good breast", even to the womb) *and* the highest and ultimate attainment in life. Both these goals should not of course be conceptualized in rigidly concrete terms but as the working out of one's sub-personalities in life and in oneself. This pair of opposites, i.e. ultimate regression and highest aim, is one important aspect both of the proprium and of the Jungian Self. However, these goals are in fact, usually and tragically, expressed in concrete terms.

The image of the rapist/robber was first produced by my patient when I was able to help him in taking an analytic attitude towards our difficulty over times. It developed into the ability to see himself as the robber/ant. I am not saying that the containing function was solely carried by me in this instance, any more than I believe that in childhood it is solely the mother who has the monopoly of the containing function in her transactions with her child. Mutual respect, devotion to the work of analysis, an understanding of the work developed over years of work together all eventually resulted in a greater ability to reach a working symbol each time a difficulty of this kind came up. Previously, we had both acted much more unconsciously, that is, more emotionally and with less understanding, but this had gradually changed in the direction of greater ability to analyse, so that more of an analytical "ego" was present each time these misunderstandings occurred, not just in me, not just in him, but in the relationship. Previously there had been a greater tendency on my part to react either passively or over-firmly in these conflict situations – these had been the only reaction possible for me at those times. And the same had been true for him, in much greater degree – he had reacted either very passively and obsequiously – or with hardness and litigiousness, reminding me of rules and principles and of things I had previously said and promised etc. His legalistic and moralizing reactions to the threats to his well-being from persecutors had figured very prominently in his social and professional behaviour in the earlier parts of his analysis, but were gradually mitigated in the way I have indicated.

When it is fully developed (if that were possible), the symbolic attitude involves giving full value to the emerging unconscious contents as well as fully recognizing their "as-if" quality. The full recognition of their "as-if" aspect involves the abandonment of primary identity and of the delusory one-ness which denies psychic reality to the other in personal relationships and to the not-me as part of the personality. In childhood it is chiefly the mother or parts of the mother with whom he at first unconsciously identifies in the boundaryless sense of primary identity. From the mother the child, we postulate, gradually learns to differentiate "himself". He separates out a self image from her image and at the same time builds bridges of communications back to her and back to his own unconscious "roots" (the parts of himself which are not differentiated out from the mother image). The symbol reaches out to the real mother and also connects him with his primary, non-differentiated self. Symbolic activity involves the giving up of these unconscious identifications, which are now felt to be delusory in character (otherwise there would be no spur towards abandoning them).

The London group of Jungian analysts has done valuable work in this field, whereby illusory or delusory identifications with the analyst can be given up and creative symbolic activity initiated. One of the first contributions was by Jackson (1963), describing an adult psychotic transference and its resolution. A little later, Dorothy Davidson (1965) described how a fantasy of being inside the analyst-mother was the beginning of her child patient's ability to give up an unconscious identification with a damaged mother image (symbolized by a blitzed site). At the same time the patient was able to deal with her envy of the idealized mother and her wish to destroy her. Many London Jungians have stressed the connection between the giving up of unconscious identification or of idealized images of togetherness or wholeness, and the acquisition of personal identity and the symbolic attitude. Among those cited in this connection by Newton (1965) are Gordon (1965), Hobson (1961), Plaut (1959) and Strauss (1964). This motif is a London variation on the theme of individuation as the separating out of the ego from the collective unconscious. The London variation makes use of the work of psychoanalysts such as Klein, Segal, Milner, Mahler and Searles (for references, see Newton 1965, 1975).

Paradoxically, this giving-up of unconscious identifications is accompanied by the creative loss of boundaries, the creative illusion, the regression to animism, underlying the formation and the sharing of symbols. Language and all human intercommunication using symbols depends on this, as well as the creative process itself.

All this work was neatly summarized by Rosemary Gordon (1967) in the sentence, "[The] transcendent function can come into operation only when the original self has been allowed to de-integrate, when uroboric union has been sacrificed and when the opposites have been constellated".

This "London" approach to symbol formation was taken further by Norah Moore (1975) with clinical examples of important stages in the ability to use symbols in adult patients. She describes this developing function as follows: If the relationship with the real mother carries enough of the experience of original wholeness, the infant is able gradually to give it up and to differentiate between "inner" and "outer". The bridge between inner and outer is at first a symbolic equivalence, but representations of the lost primal self may then occur. As the ego develops, it defends itself against the unconscious from which it is emerging, but also relates to it by participating in the transcendent function. Later on, the formed ego is able to be an observer because defences have developed, and it has now to make some effort to get in touch with the unconscious, as in active imagination.

In times of regression, the unconscious is all around without much barrier, and no special effort is needed to encounter it. The symbol forms a bridge between inner and outer, relating always to the wholeness of the self. The conscious mind reaches out to whatever is unknown to it, whether in the unconscious or without, where the inner images are met as projections.

Thus the transcendent function is first encountered as a projective mechanism, which gives way later to creative formulation and imagination; the experience of the opposites is at first discontinuous, but later the opposites confront one another and a capacity for ambivalence develops. The developing transcendent function forms a bridge between the opposites as they collide; the gap between real and imaginary widens; here the symbol is born; it allows conscious and unconscious to take hold of each other in a coniunctio at once tangible and infinite.

In summary, it might be said that the symbol reaches out to an original wholeness, a primary identity, a delusion of oneness, and also reaches out to adaptation to reality, to the other person, to the not-me part of the Self. It tends to occur precisely when the delusion of unity is (through the experiences of oneness and also of conflict) being given up. This "giving up" is often accompanied by considerable anger, the anger of frustrated omnipotence. One usually learns to cope with this anger and pain by using the example of respected persons who have already learned to do so.

But it is not just a matter of foregoing blissful one-ness with the idealized mother, matrix, analyst or anima figure. It is equally a matter of separating from the dead or damaged mother or Other, the blitzed site, the dead lover etc. And that is the liberating aspect of separation. Paradoxically, the patient is only able to give up his delusory one-ness when the delusory one-ness, the infantile omnipotence, of the patient is given enough value by the analyst. It seems to be a fundamental law of analysis, perhaps of parenting and of human relationships in general, that the individual (patient, infant etc.) can only yield up his pertinent bit of unconsciousness when this bit is given (or maybe feels it is given) enough recognition, value, sympathy (exactly which and what varies of course) by the analyst, parent etc. This is the essence of the effective countertransference attitude which has to be worked on by the analyst in connection with unconscious aspects of himself as well as of his patient. I hope this was made clear in the example I gave from my own work.

In this chapter on the symbolic attitude I have confined myself largely to a synopsis of the London contribution on symbols in relation to the transference and the developing ego. There are many considerations I have omitted which have been emphasized by Jung himself as well as by workers in other schools of psychology. For instance, as I write

I am watching two kittens at play on the hearth-rug, "playing at" stalking their prey, fighting their enemies, fleeing from danger etc. All these things they have never actually done. Their claws have never been extended in anger, their teeth have never closed on an enemy, they have never been really frightened by any real danger, they "fight" and pat each other with a delicacy which is always fun for each other. It is obvious that an "as-if" element has to be there from the start (in practice rather than in the conscious awareness of the kittens). The reaction of the mother cat or of the other kitten may be important in modifying the playful attacks as they occur. The human infant is the same. He never seriously sets about devouring the breast. Similarly, the most delinquent child, as well as the most fanatical witch-doctor, does not *actually* behave like a lion even though he "knows" himself to be one. In other words, the nature of play and of the inhibitory functions and boundaries which eventually result in adult symbolic activity are far more complex than the above formulations suggest. But these formulations are based on clinically important changes in our patients as they develop the symbolic attitude. Furthermore, they are useful to our trainees, and work done by our trainees on their control cases in recent years has shown a deep understanding and ability to use these ideas, with gratifying changes in their patients and their patients' relationships with their inner lives.

My own contribution (Redfearn, 1965, 1970, 1973, 1978, 1980, 1982) has mainly concerned the integration of the subjective body and the mind in the symbolic experience, and of the role of the therapist in holding the opposites in the sense used above. This has involved training oneself in the use of the feelings and experiencing their basis in bodily experience, particularly in countertransference feelings and impulses. One uses oneself as a sensitized instrument in the work of paying attention to the patient. I do not claim to be alone, or even a pioneer, in this area. It is all very much part of the stock-in-trade of modern analysis, at least of the London Jungians and of many or most psychonalysts too. But to illustrate what I mean let me give another everyday example of this sort of skill, this time from work with a young professional man.

In a recent session we were discussing my custom of charging for missed sessions, even when he had to miss them because of his work, and even when he gave me ample advance notice. He felt this to be unduly rigid, and said that he was much more flexible with *his* clients. I certainly saw his point and we agreed to talk over the matter further.

At the next session, to my interest, he did not bring up the subject, but instead he said he wanted to be more disciplined in his life and his work. He spent evenings in the bath instead of preparing work for his students next day. He needed pressure to make him work – pressure of time or the pressure of guilt. Once he had succeeded in getting into a working frame of mind he could not stop. If he stopped, he became ill.

So he needed self-discipline in order to be able to start work and also in order to be able to stop work and avoid overworking.

He continued in the same vein about his inability to write scientific papers. When trying to do so, he makes tea, goes for walks, needs the stimulus of dialogue, is unable to do it himself. He had masses of material, had invented his own innovative method of working professionally which was found invaluable by his trainees, but had not managed to publish a single paper about it. He had got into a similar difficulty with his doctorate thesis at university. The masses of material he accumulated simply got out of hand, so that he could not substantiate his brilliant ideas which gave him grandiose fantasies and feelings of genius.

I replied to this by saying there seemed to be a difficulty in gripping, grasping, biting and digesting his material and his mental contents and that he needed to fight them every inch of the way down on to the paper. Instead, he let the material swallow him. I said there seemed to be an inhibitory force at work inhibiting the full and free use of his hands, nails and teeth. He said that seemed exactly right. He then remembered a dream of the night before of torturing a woman to death by scratching and tearing the skin off her with his nails, and biting her.

On his way out, he said that he wondered why we had not discussed fees during the session, as we had hoped. I said jokingly that he needed to scratch and tear at me and that maybe we could discuss fees some more soon when he had done that.

My interpretation about the inhibition of hands and teeth was based on my own bodily impulses and sensations when he was outlining his difficulties in coping with his own mental contents, in particular his inability to write papers.

This young man was at the end of his first year of twice-a-week analysis and we had achieved a good working relationship in which at least at times his dreams, the transference–countertransference relationship, the bodily impulses and sensations and mental metaphors of the therapist, and the symbolic experiences were all being interpreted and seemed to be very much at the same psychic level. This occurs when the working relationship is in some sense a primal relationship where symbolic, archetypal experience and bodily experience are not split off from each other.

To a large extent this skill can be learned. It is obviously a skill not just of the analyst but of the relationship. But trainee analysts can be taught to learn this skill in their analytical relationships. For example, if a trainee in supervision with me says his client hurt him when he said so-and-so, he is encouraged to notice what sort of hurt it felt like and where the hurt was experienced. Was it a stabbing, a scathing, a crushing or whatever kind of attack etc.? Training can help us use attacks on our narcissism to our own and the client's advantage, and our interpretations are directed towards helping the client to realize why he attacks in these ways. The same use is made of positive affects which are reflected back to the client in a similar way. All this sounds far more systematic and deliberate than it actually is. Emphasizing just one aspect of the work is responsible for this.

This working relationship in analysis is referred to by Winnicot (1971) as an area of mutual play, in the sense that client and analyst are each giving the other the necessary space in which creative activity can occur, and each can use the space between subjective and "objective" reality, illusion and "reality", in a creative way. The approach and the theoretical formulation of the London Group of analytical psychologists owe a good deal to our proximity to Winnicott and the Tavistock Clinic. This gives a peculiar flavour to the London kind of Jungian teaching, which this present volume tries to convey.

Chapter Nine

Boundaries and mandalas

If I have shown nothing else, I hope I have shown so far in this book that we are not one person but many, although some people are more one person than others. Our feeling of "I", as well as our behaviour, is being competed for and dominated by our various selves, one of which is in charge at one time, another at another.

From the present point of view it does not matter in a very vital way what we call these functioning selves within ourselves. Following Jung, we can call them archetypes and complexes, attempting thereby to distinguish between the collective and the personal elements, while admitting the difficulties that this involves. Following Freud, we can describe the main elements in structural terms, ego, id, super-ego etc., while deriving these elements partly from the personal experiences of the individual concerned. Or we may derive our basic personality elements from experience of parts of ourselves and our parents and other people, or whole-person experiences which become functioning personalities within ourselves. This would be stressed by analysts using object-relations theory.

To me it is obvious that all these sources of experience enter into these selves within ourselves. Sometimes we are taken over by an "introjected parent" within ourselves, but this has obvious archetypal roots and overtones, and is perhaps, for example, heavily influenced by some powerful experience we had even as late as our teens or adult lives. There is not so much argument in practice about the origin in a patient of a particular unconscious figure which constitutes an important sub-personality among analysts and therapists as there might be thought to be by theoreticians – students and academic psychologists who can afford the luxury of remaining clear-headed about such things, and who have not lost their intellectual virginity.

Because there are so many competing ideas about the sources and origins of these persons within our personality, and yet general agreement about their clinical and social importance, and because of the way they function as incomplete persons yet as persons in the same sense as the characters in a play function, I think my term "sub-personality" deserves to be taken up for general use. It deserves use simply because it is a non-sectarian term and because these clinically important part-selves that we meet in ourselves, in others and in social phenomena are living characters within ourselves and must be met as such. John's "lion" behaviour and his lion symbol in the last chapter was archetypal, was complex-determined, had oral sadistic elements (part-object psychology) and, no doubt, had introjected maternal and paternal elements. Freud might even have said the lion "stood for" the father or something of that sort. The use of any current term such as complex or archetype or internal part-object for the lion is needlessly controversial at the clinical level, where what matters is recognizing and meeting the "lion" bit of John. I am all for controversy but only when it is to the point. In practice, therapists use such terms as "the lion bit of John" etc. to convey our meaning in a non-controversial way, and this kind of terminology serves very well among clinical workers of various schools. The use of a term like "lion bit", however, leaves one open to the possibility of not being taken seriously. What self-respecting psychology lecturer could use the term "lion bit" in his learned articles? Perhaps he might however be able to use the term "'lion' sub-personality".

A sub-personality, like a character in a play, can sometimes be seen to be a personified mood, vice or part object (e.g. all-giving breast or all-accepting lavatory, or archetype (e.g. good mother, bad father or an environmental introject (e.g. teenage idol or cult figure). Or it could be a personality feature developed in reaction to an environmental pressure. A complete classification of sub-personalities and their inter-relationship within ourselves would be a catalogue of our dreams and symbolic activity, as well as a complete account of our predominant behaviours and of the culture of our time.

The notion of sub-personality is sufficiently close to characters in a play to make it advisable to remind the reader that it also includes important features in the scenery or setting. A glowering landscape, a pastoral idyll, a blasted heath, a limitless sea, a rock in the sea, a ship, a motor car or a house, all would come under the heading of sub-personalities. It is these apparently inhuman, impersonal or supra-personal elements which make one wonder whether the term sub-personality is the most appropriate one. A splendid house or a stubborn rock, yes, these can without difficulty be felt as types of person, roles or behaviours, but some of the other scenario-type sub-personalities require a little more imagination. Yet this sort of imagination is needed if dreams are to be discussed and interpreted and the image within them understood as aspects of oneself. An even greater difficulty lies in the fact that some sub-personalities transcend the "I" and are subjectively superior, even vastly superior, to the conscious "I".

If all one's sub-personalities were spread out like a map or landscape, or a vast world of happenings and relationships, there would be places or scenes which were often visited by the conscious "I", and others which would never have been visited, or have even been avoided. The feeling of "I", as I have so often pointed out, may inhabit one role for a moment, then another. Other roles might be avoided especially in certain circumstances. Some people are stuck in one role much of the time, especially if that role has paid dividends in the past. And we talk of the "persona" as a description of our favoured social role or roles.

Granted that we are all many (and how can we avoid granting that?) can I be one? (Jung, 1955/1956, p. 8, Footnote 26).

Happily I do not often experience myself as a bundle of competing, co-operating or conflicting persons – or as a bundle of reflexes, instincts and emotional habits for that matter. Sometimes I do feel more fragmented, sometimes more of a piece. Usually I feel that I exist, that I and people and things are real, that I am continuous with the person I was in the past as far back as I can remember, that I matter to myself and others, that I am good and bad (mostly good), more often depressed than elated etc. The way "I" feel about "myself" varies but is a kind of probability system of habits. To a certain extent it is another way of describing which of my sub-personalities is most often in charge of, or inhabited by, my "I". This is not to deny how important it is how one feels about oneself.

Often the "I" feeling is possessed by one sub-personality of a pair in a complex, and the "myself" by the other of the same pair. A patient of mine had a critical father. She often berates herself as the father berated her. She talks to herself as if she were the father talking to her. Sometimes she the father approves of herself and then the world is a very different place. Sometimes the "I" is the daughter projecting the critical or the approving father on to authority figures in the real world. All these vicissitudes of the "I" and "myself" are commonly encountered in what we call a "father complex". Of course, much of the time there is not such a clear boundary between the "I" and the "myself". Bollas (1982) has worked out beautifully how some of these sub-personalities operate in relation to each other, using a development of object-relations theory. Where a complex is at work, the "I" and the "myself" are sometimes possessed by the two sub-personalities comprising the complex. The sub-personalities in question may reverse roles so that the one possessing the "I" may possess the "myself" or the "other" (externally experienced person or thing), while the one possessing the "myself" now possesses the "I". All this sounds more complicated than it is in practice, once one is accustomed to identifying sub-personalities. I remember the panic-stricken confusion I was in in my first practical histology class in medical school. Through the microscope I could see nothing of the tissues and structures I was supposed to see. It was all a confused mass. The demonstrator patiently pointed out the elements on the slide, where they were in the field of vision, and what their shape and colour were. It is just the same in bird-spotting and in sub-personality spotting. Sub-personality naming may be a useful exercise and lead to a saving of time in subsequent sessions. Sub-personality spotting involves identifying important dream symbols and relating them to the behaviour of the patient, to his feelings about various things and people including of course the analyst, to his past and to his present problems.

Vicissitudes of the "I" in a Person with Sado-masochistic Fantasies

In order to illustrate the concept of shifts in the location of the "I" from one sub-personality to another in the terrain of the personality as a whole, I shall describe various I-states in a patient who at the beginning of treatment suffered from, and enjoyed, sexual fantasies in which she was a little girl, or as if a little girl was being beaten or otherwise ill-treated or dominated by a powerful male figure. In her conscious life she was under the powerful influence of the complex on frequent occasions. When carried away by the logic of an idea, by professional zeal or by the need to make a point, she was possessed by the dominant male part of the complex, and in therapy sessions I the analyst then felt crushed or subdued, unheard etc. I might rally myself or feel annoyed, and insist on being heard. If I did this with sufficient forcefulness she then became the subdued and hurt one.

We may say in this case that her sado-masochistic complex was composed of two complementary sub-personalities, the dominant male and the hurt little girl victim. The fact that a "complex" existed meant that there was a marked tendency for one of the pair of sub-personalities or the other to be very readily activated, and for the pattern of the former sexual fantasy to be metaphorically lived out, albeit most unwillingly, by my patient – not literally of course, and not with any awareness of sexual excitement, but in a none the less real way (as far as feelings of domination and being hurt were concerned, as felt by me, the analyst).

Her feeling of "I" was therefore associated first with the dominant male sub-personality with its respective motives, attitudes, bodily impulses etc. Then, if I over-reacted or retaliated, her feeling of "I" was associated with the hurt little girl sub-personality. Her behaviour was in the same sense controlled first from one of the sub-personalities of the complex, then from the other. She was subject to moods which were due to the predominance of one of the sub-personalities or the other – in one mood unhappy and vulnerable, in the other competent, efficient and practical.

Her paintings, which were essentially self-representations and over which she had virtually no conscious control, were at one time either vulnerable and beset by demands and impingements or highly protected with bright colours and sharp boundaries. Some of these paintings were like bright eggs with very strong and sharp boundaries. They corresponded with the dominant sub-personalities. Others were vulnerable and invaded right to their centres by red colour etc. Later, there was a series of tree paintings with strong roots, trunk and branches, the red colour entering the roots and acting like sap, feeding and vitalizing the whole. By then considerable work had been done on the complex and its interpretation. The tree corresponded with the growth of a normal healthy feeling of "I".

How do we define her boundaries or her ego-boundaries when she was a person divided into a too sharply defined sub-personality and a too easily hurt sub-personality? Like the rest of us, she had other sub-personalities which possessed or partially controlled her at other times, and I have mentioned two only of her important ones. Each important sub-personality has its own boundary or set of boundaries. This would also include a corresponding set of attitudes and affective predispositions with their corresponding sets of body armouring (defensive blockages, zones of tension etc.).

It is worth recording in passing that my patient was never the dominant male in her sexual fantasy, and that she had great difficulty in seeing herself as in any way a dominant male figure. This sub-personality was in this sense part of the "shadow", but when she was "possessed" or "controlled" by it she was cheerful, competent and more her normal self than when controlled by the hurt little girl. Her paintings were bright when they represented the "normal" side, dark when they represented the "hurt" side.

The advantage of using the term "sub-personality" for both the strong male and the hurt female figures is clear. Both figures are "archetypal" in that they occur in many myths, fairy tales, religious symbols, etc., yet they were very personal and very much part of her peculiar personal history and real life traumata. The term sub-personality describes exactly how these figures act and begs no theoretical questions about "innate" and "acquired". Both terms, archetype and internal object, are as it were trying to argue a point instead of simply describing the phenomena.

If my patient had been able to overcome her hurt feelings more "successfully", she might have been more permanently controlled by the dominant male part of herself. In this sense she would have had a more stable and definite character with more stable and definite boundaries. People more "stuck" in one sub-personality have in this sense more of a tendency to have well-defined boundaries. But they are I think physically less healthy than my patient, who was eventually able to integrate these two sides of herself.

If one's "I" or one's "self" may be possessed or inhabited by different sub-personalities, often opposite in nature (such as dominant male and hurt female), at different times, does this not make a nonsense of what we call a person's "personality" or "character"? In the case of my patient who was tormented by sado-masochistic sexual fantasies, she was thought to be overbearing in some social situations and would have been described as overbearing by people who only knew her in those situations, e.g. work situations. In some other situations, e.g. domestic situations, she was mostly a cheerful, sensible mother, and sometimes a clinging, irritable little girl towards her husband.

These statements of the obvious are not intended to deny the usefulness of descriptions of personality and character. For example, if I say that such-and-such a person is a narcissistic depressive, and suffers from a feeling of "no-one loves me as I need to be loved", I am saying a great deal about him, his probable childhood experience of his mother or parents, and about the type of sub-personality most likely to be possessing his "I" most of the time. We can also make a pretty good guess which of complementary sub-personalities are likely to be in charge under different circumstances. If we say so-and-so is lacking in self-confidence, we are saying that his "I" is usually possessed by an under-valued sub-personality and that the complementary sub-personality which may occasionally possess him is likely to be grandiose, infantile and undifferentiated. In other words, a description of character is simply a description of the sub-personalities most likely to be in charge, and when and under what circumstances they may reverse roles, etc. Every man is supposed to have his price, and likewise there are circumstances in most men under which his normally encountered sub-personalities may reverse roles or be displaced.

To be able to say "I feel like that little girl I dreamt of the other day" or "I am behaving like that obnoxious little boy I keep dreaming about" or "There I go again repeating that role" requires a good deal of sophistication and insight. Often it is a matter of "I feel awful" or "the bastard is at it again, bullying everybody around". The "I" is usually not prominent and if so is taken for granted. The "sub-personality in charge" is experienced in terms of the emotion or affect being experienced. How do these sub-personalities relate to the "I"? The sub-personalities are of the same general nature as Jung's complexes and archetypes. I only use the word "sub-personality" because in practice it is difficult or impossible to sort out the complex component from the archetypal component in a given dream figure or "internal object", e.g. a lion or a sadistic male figure.

This is not the same thing as asserting that it is always divisive or counterproductive to attempt to distinguish between the concept of archetype and the concept of the internal object, or to attempt to sort out how much of the one and how much of the other is operative in any particular clinical case or instance. But knowing how difficult it is in practice to sort out "personal" and "collective" or "universal" elements as contributory factors, psychoanalysts consider it presumptuous to use, as a matter of routine, terms which besides denoting these very real and empirically important parts of the self also simultaneously presume to "explain" them exclusively the one way or the other.

There is an additional complication in that the important sub-personalities include something like Freud's super-ego and id, and the various parts of the personality corresponding to Freud's stages of psycho-sexual development. Sometimes one of these may be important clinically, sometimes another. In actual biographies and case histories sometimes Jung's schemata seem more appropriate, sometimes Freud's etc. Hence my preference for a relatively non-specific term which describes the main dream symbols, behavioural patterns, personal interaction and aspects of the "I–Self relationship", occurring either sequentially in an analysis or at any one time in the life of a person.

Enriching of the "I" and of the Sense of Self

What happens to my "I" feeling when I integrate a bit of my personality which was previously unconscious, acted out etc. in the manner described in the last chapter?

Let us go back to "John lion". He became aware, let us say, of a "lion" part of himself that was restless and unsatisfied and wanted to attack people including the analyst, of a "cage" part of himself, of a "lead" part of himself, of a part that cared for the analyst and wanted to protect her from the lion etc. He became aware of and able to cope with these potentially conflicting and ambivalent parts of himself and able to make a game or scenario in which the problems were worked out. The game was the representation of the enrichment and differentiation of his "I" and of his self-image. Previously he had felt unsatisfied, restless, anxious (for the mother figure) and afraid. And in a very important sense unaware of the lion in himself, perhaps merely aware of wanting to attack.

"I" and "self" are enriched and strengthened more or less *pari passu* in this example. The opposing feelings of hate and love are integrated by means of the game or, rather, into the game. Stories, myths, fairy tales etc. are the means, or the representations, of the method, whereby the opposites are experienced and resolved in a meaningful enantiodroma.

When experienced in this personal way, they represent a personal enrichment and strengthening. Our cultural heritage is a tapestry of such enrichments.

Experiences of Unity. The Mandala as a Symbol of a Super-ordinate Selfness and Unity

I am not proposing to describe laboriously the emergence in the infant of the "I" and of self-awareness in infancy. I refer the reader to the works of Erikson, Mahler, Winnicott, Kohut and Spitz, for example, and, for a summary of a "London" Jungian viewpoint, to an article by Lambert (1981). Much of this work is speculative as far as generalizations are concerned. Instead, I should like to confine myself to certain experiential aspects of I-experience, bodily well-being, successful defences, and with Jung's concept of the self and of the mandala as a symbol of wholeness. It is assumed that the reader is familiar with Jung's work on the self.

The ability to experience oneself as a closed circle suggests a certain feeling of intactness and security, a certain resilience. Mention was made in Chapter 4 of a one-year-old child described by Michael Fordham who was able to sally forth as a free person, forsaking the protection of a grown-up and at the same time draw a circle. In his *Memories, Dreams, Reflections*, Jung (1963) describes his own painting and drawings of mandalas as he found his own identity and self-hood after the break with Freud.

That the days on which his mandala showed intact defences were days on which he was able to deny his vulnerability is suggested by the shattering effect on his mandala when he received a letter from a patient to whom he was susceptible. To me this would be Jung's salvation and proof of his humanity, as opposed to his being a closed system. However, it is often possible to exhibit more flexible and adaptive boundaries than Jung had at that time, so that one is neither continent and closed, nor shattered and incontinent. The mandala may then take on a more human form.

In the last chapter I described how the "I" can be felt to be located inside or outside a barrier which represents a defensive system (the one threatened by the robber ant). If the "I" is felt to be inside the circle, we have a (paranoid) situation in which the bad is "successfully" placed outside; and if the "I" is outside, we have a situation of envy in which the good thing or good experience is felt to be unattainable. The two situations are the two sides of a coin. My patient tended to swing (or rather click) from the one to the other, until he learned to feel and give, give and take, relax his boundaries etc.

Denials, reversals and transformations take place as the boundary, the envy barrier as one might call it, is crossed. Pregenital, repressed "id" impulses may be experienced in the bad form (e.g. oral sadism) outside the barrier, and in a good form on the other side of the barrier. In a short article (Redfearn, 1974), I showed how one patient's oral sadistic impulses were transformed into various idealized images incorporated into her mandalas which she was painting at the time (e.g. flowers). Thus the mandala represented her waking self, a defensive system in which the split-off impulses were transformed, idealized, appropriated into the self-feeling, and in short became part of the "ego-defences" of the patient. The transformation, reversal, idealization and "adultization" of infantile-sexual or other "shadow" impulses as they cross the "envy-barrier", "ego boundary" or the mandala boundary suggest a fundamental law of the self. It can be stated as follows. A shadow part of the Self is warded off by a corresponding and opposing idealized portion of self. The zone of interaction has boundary qualities and is symbolized by barriers. When the feeling "I" is located on the "wrong" side of the barrier, we have a situation of envy. Thus a "strong" boundary or barrier is always accompanied by a corresponding envious, attacking or deprived impulse or fantasy in the "not-I" (the unconscious). This envy is of course usually projected on to others. Of course, the more pairs of opposites which are experienced as part of the self or which are reconciled within the mandala, the more we can say the self approximates to the Self or total personality.

Thus my patient's envious oral sadistic impulses (towards men, ultimately towards her mother-image) which she felt when excluded or left out, were normally defended against by loving, generous, giving feelings which she felt towards her children and her analyst, and which were represented by flowers at the periphery of her first mandalas, which were transformed teeth and mouths.

The patient awoke from a dream in which she was escaping from a wood by crushing the skull of an opposing person by stepping on it. As she awoke, she had an image of a sun or bright disc which was a precursor of her mandala images. Thus the boundaries of the wood of her dream represent such a boundary between a self and a not-self in her personality at that time. These boundaries are not strictly speaking ego-boundaries, boundaries of the "myself" or of the feeling of self, nor of course are they boundaries of the Self in the sense of total personality or of total potential awareness. Yet they are important and they are to do with the self. Mandalas are self-representations in an important sense, as Jung has more than amply demonstrated.

Some mandalas have very thick walls suggesting impregnable defences. That is what they are, or that is what it is hoped they are. Defences against what? The answer is obviously against some "shadow" part of the personality projected into the not-self; in religious mandalas, often against evil forces. Not all evil is contained along with good inside the mandala, or transformed into neutral energy inside the system. Strong defences are only needed against strong "not-self" forces. They need to be abandoned or even breached. They correspond with the person's rigidity and hardness. The nature and rigidity of the defences is determined primarily in the early years of life, but they can be altered by analysis, and a Jungian analysis is essentially a character analysis when we reach these levels of the self.

However, Jung himself did not describe how important the analyst may be in the emergence of the self in the sense of that which is represented or symbolized by the mandala. The presence of the analyst as a caring, validating parental being may be necessary for a spell, even for years, for the selfness as represented by the mandala to be established and to be able to survive without the analyst. For example, for many years my sado-masochistic patient had no feeling of mattering or counting either to herself or anyone else. Indeed, she could not paint at all unless I was real to her. My reality faded within a day or two so that frequent sessions were important, and holidays resulted in a set-back of many weeks in our work, in her sense of having anyone there and of being a person. By the time she could paint a tree, a sense of a self that mattered was developing, but this too depended on the continuity in our relationship for some time. The roots disappeared when I went on holiday. The tree is of course a self-representation in a similar sense to the mandala – the mandala is the tree in cross section so to speak. Both represent the self as a unity stretching into the past and into the unconscious as well as into the heights.

This is not the result of an isolated clinical experience with one patient. I have confirmed the relationship of self-feeling and the transference relationship repeatedly, as have many colleagues. It must have been known to Jung but is rather neglected by him in his published work. There is an important bridge here with Kohut's work.

I should like to return to the patient in my last chapter who tended to react to changes in his life or arrangements as if they were attacks by an invasive robber attacking his defences. He later had an experience when he was the invasive robber (the ant trying to get to the primal scene/womb/the treasure hard to attain). But his ant-self is prevented from getting to the treasure by a thick wall. He experiences at this time a left-out, envious feeling which makes him feel like screaming. But what is stopping him getting to the treasure, to the happiness he seeks? Nothing but his own defences, his fear of being robbed or raped, his persecution complex, now experienced in projection as the thick wall. To realize this is a great step forward in an analysis, as the reader might easily imagine. To be able to experience, really *experience*, both sides of the wall, that is a new and dearly won bit of wholeness; when deeply felt and realized, these are very moving times in an analysis.

In this patient we have a mandala with a treasure at the centre, surrounded by a thick wall. A robber is attacking this wall. It is not surprising that this patient spent a lot of his energies in beautifying and strengthening his house, securing his financial position, defending his professional status, and worrying about his bodily health. In all these roles his feelings of self were on the inside of the mandala, whose wall was being threatened from outside. What was he worrying about? He was worrying about being poor, left out, deprived, a needy, greedy baby who could not ever get to the breast in its fullest and richest sense. But this is what he was; this he felt like a good deal of the time, in fact. The robber was none but his needy self, the riches were likewise himself and his own richness and generosity. But there is no terminology involving ego, self and defences in any fixed sense which does justice to the shifts of "I" feeling over and across this boundary wall. Nevertheless, the boundary was very real and is the most important thing clinically in the whole character.

When he felt rich, valued, sufficed, loved, for example after making love, the wall was not there. Richness and generosity prevailed and there was less have-not feeling, less envy. The ant had attained the treasure, the baby was fed, for the time being. But these were not very frequent or prevalent feelings on the whole. Usually the treasure was what the other person had or what of his the other person was trying to steal, the previous faeces-babies he wanted to give to his father, and which the father had extracted from him by force (metaphorically speaking) in his childhood.

Yet whether "he" was the owner of the treasure, the treasure itself, the guardian wall, the guardian of the treasure or the robber/ant, he felt himself to be himself, that is, a continuous being with memories going back to childhood of himself as the same person. This basic continuity and unity as a person is of course under threat at times in us all, and seems to be a feeling or experience acquired by the infant from the early relationship with the mother. It can be shattered and possibly the first rage is felt subjectively by the infant as a breaking up of this continuity. In a different way it is broken up when the baby does not feel held or supported. It accumulates good contents and expels bad feelings in a paranoid way until it feels strong and secure. Then it can afford to be magnanimous and responsible and caring. Then it can have a separate existence and sacrifice things for others and have symbolic experiences and a mental life. We see the child growing up in this way; the child experiences "himself" growing up in this way.

Returning to the diagram of central treasure, surrounding wall and ant, our terminological confusion, that which we hoped to avoid in

Chapter 1, seems to be complete. His feeling of "I" or "myself" could certainly be located inside or outside the wall and also in the wall itself. It is equally certain that the system of wall and contained treasure which is a mandala, cannot be said to represent the conscious self or the Self, for the following reasons:

(1) It is not always the subjective "I". The "I" can be located in other parts of the personality not represented in this system at all.
(2) It does not represent the subjective self or "I" which is an experience of continuity over the life of the individual.
(3) It does not represent the total personality because sometimes the wall is felt not to be there at all.

It might represent a feeling of totality or wholeness on occasions, and certainly the treasure indicates an aspiration towards completeness and happiness. But the wall was usually felt to be weak and the defences under threat when the "I" was located within the wall. He was much of the time feeling under threat of invasion, robbery, depletion, abandonment etc. The treasure–wall–ant diagram, in spite of all this, represented an extremely important statement about his character and defences. The nearest words to designate what it represents are "complex relating to the individual's sense of self". Here "complex" is used in the Jungian sense. At any one moment, and often for periods of hours or even days, it was an accurate self-representation, which was left behind and returned to (in an altered form) frequently in the spiral of development and in the vicissitudes of the changes of mood and the circumstances of daily living. The diagram importantly represented his "proprium" or his self-concept but only when his persecution complex (treasure or defences under threat or felt to be breached) or his envy (ant feelings, left-out feelings) were activated. His persecution complex and his envy were the two sides of the coin of this basic complex. But this complex was not by any means always the dominant feature of his behaviour, even of his way of relating to others, which was usually normal and open.

But a symbol which represents the goal of life, the primal scene, and the womb all at the same time can hardly be said to be peripheral or not vitally important. We cannot be dealing with anything but a central or core complex. Jung's work on mandalas suggests a quite central importance. The circle in its perfection, roundness, continuity and sealing-off quality must represent feelings which are vitally important at times, feelings of security, completeness and independence. But what about the other aspects of the mandala which Jung describes in the individuation process, namely, its four-fold character, and its quality as a symbol of reconciled opposites, and of mental functioning balanced between the four functions of thinking, feeling, sensation and intuition (see for example Jung, 1944, pp. 91–213)? I must confess that when there is order, harmony and symmetry in a picture by a patient, I tend to look for what is left out and what is happening in the personal life of the patient at the time. In particular, the ugliness, squalor and the many banal and ordinary aspects of life and death are not to be ignored and not to be despised even as sources of life, vigour and enjoyment. For example, the patient who painted the beautiful mandalas described in my article on mandala symbols (Redfearn, 1974) painted quite a few messy "faecal" pictures afterwards, and then spent a lot of analytical effort in getting more into her own body and then into her paranoid defences. But this is not to deny the validity of mandala symbolism and its importance at certain stages of analysis: it is probable that for all stages of development there is a mandala which includes more complex opposites and more profound opposites. Rotation is an important change when it occurs and is meaningful. And in any case symbols of harmony and creativity are clinically of importance when they occur as new phenomena in, say, a patient for whom the "primal scene" is a sadistic one, a warring one, a non-creative one, one in which the partners are fused and not separate, one in which gloom overhangs all etc. In such people good and creative interaction between opposites symbolized as happening inside a container, which represents the self in an important sense, can be an unforgettable landmark in an analysis.

One patient for whom the achievement of a balanced tetramorphic mandala was a particularly important stage in her analysis was a woman with pronounced weakness and underdevelopment of her left leg due to poliomyelitis at the age of five. Some of her early "mandalas" were very asymmetrical with a missing or undifferentiated left lower quarter, corresponding to a distorted body-image and bodily self-image. A symmetrical harmonious "self" as opposed to a grossly asymmetrical body-image was in her case something to be won after great struggle and much analysis. The symmetrical mandala was achieved at about the same time that rotation of the mandala became a prominent feature. Rotation of the mandala, or rotation of the "I" position around the centre, is an indication of movement and flexibility of comparable importance to the movement of the "I" across the boundaries or the merging which may result in a creative depression analogous to the nigredo of the alchemists (see Jung, 1944, 1946).

But sometimes rotation is too rapid for consciousness to follow. For example, a patient of mine with a sado-masochistic father complex dreamt on coming into analysis of his father cutting off the head of a cockerel in the scullery. This was followed by an image of a catherine-wheel firework display of great intensity. The patient left analysis, "cured", before the complex could be thoroughly worked through in the transference-countertransference relationship.

The existence of a complex means that the "I" of the individual concerned becomes drawn towards each component of the complex, usually more often towards one rather than another. In the example of the son made timid by a frightening, dominating father, his "I" will be drawn towards the "timid child" side of the complex, as if towards a magnet. Occasionally his "I" will be possessed by the dominating father. But the point I am trying to make at present is that our complexes are competing for our "I" feeling and for control of our behaviour, and are trying to keep us unconscious, whereas there are opposite tendencies, tendencies towards consciousness and choice, subsumed under the heading of individuating tendencies, and first described in detail by Jung.

When one or both parents have been possessive, the square or circle may represent the limits of permitted self-expression within which the "I" is imprisoned. One such patient of mine dreamt early in analysis of being kept prisoner inside a square of neatly cut lawn by a savage dog which dragged him back if he tried to escape. The dog represented his mother's reactions to his attempts at freedom, the square of lawn the narrow limits of his ability to show himself, display his feelings or potency – be himself. Sometimes the boundary is a prison wall, at other times experienced in a positive, womb-like sense. The maternal container-boundary is also felt as a boundary of the self containing naughty or good impulses or parts of the personality (another example of the "I" being at one time located inside the boundary, at another time at the boundary).

I think that most of our normal, ordinary, everyday, adaptive mental functioning is carried on without much of a feeling of "I", without narcissistic involvement, that is, no doubt. Complexes are "I"-magnets, and usually involve boundaries which are zones of prohibition, inhibition or containment (these are not necessarily meant in a purely negative or pejorative sense here). If the "I" crosses such a boundary we are dealing with a change of affect, mood or role. Powerful boundaries involve unconscious (projected) envy with feelings of vulnerability or persecution, or conscious envious attempts to break them down (envious attacks on an idealized internal or "external" object).

The analyst sometimes constellates the opposite or "other" part of the complex for the patient for a time, but gradually, he hopes, he is able to help the patient contain these opposites to some degree. At first it may be a merely intellectual appreciation of his different roles or "selves", but this is at least an important beginning. Concern and responsibility for both parts of the Self in question are necessary for conscious choice to begin to be made.

Chapter Ten

Conclusion

This book has to be concluded, in spite of no conclusions being reachable on its subject matter.

As regards its title, I do not think there is much difficulty in the idea that there are many selves present in us all, which I have presumed to call sub-personalities, and which I liken to the many characters in a play which corresponds with the total person. My main contribution to this subject, it seems to me, is to avoid using words for these sub-personalities which take sides over matters about which there is no point in arguing all the time, although every point in arguing *some* of the time. For instance, such terms as "archetypes" and "internal objects" overlap in clinical practice, and the images and characters in our dreams and our personalities can never be said to be purely one thing or another, although they are important, powerful, energetic, the very stuff of life in fact. The notion of the feeling of "I", and of behaviour, moving about from one sub-personality to another, is perhaps a little more difficult in practice, as it takes an outside view of the personality. Subjectively, it does not feel like that. It is the outside observer who can see this more easily than the subject whose "I" usually feels of a piece, continuous with the past and embodied in one's body and so on. But the notions of "possession" and "multiple personalities" are, in my opinion only extreme examples of an essentially normal and normally essential de-integrative dynamic which goes with any adaptation or need for either behaviour or reflection.

It is the self as a subjective unity, a relatively stable concept, the object of valuation and judgement, which presents more conceptual difficulties. Of anything we can say about it, the opposite can easily be shown to be true. This applies even more to the Jungian Self which I have written about particularly in Chapters 2 and 9.

For example, the self is to do with the individual but is completely dependent on his relationships – originally the relationship with the mother. Even in adults there is a level which one often reaches in analysis where the essential attributes of continuity, meaningfulness, mattering, harmony etc. mean the analysand or the analyst in an interchangeable sense. The two are not distinguishable *vis-à-vis* the self at this level.

Again, this self has "defences", needs for security, ideals and goals. Yet these very "defences" and goals are obstacles and barriers to the "I" that is struggling to reach his heart's desire. This self has to do with unity, uniting and relating to the breast, the womb and the deepest regressive wishes (the circle); but it is also to do with separation, differentiation, the ability to maintain boundaries clear and inviolate, the functions of analysing and thinking (the square, the Cross etc.) Light and darkness, love and hate, good and bad, infinitesimal and infinite, form and colour, what opposites can we omit as fundamental in connection with the self and the Self? Two opposites which are worth mentioning are the manifestations of "infantile sexuality" and their transformed, culturally idealized, symbolic counterparts. The mysteries of these transformations have been very sketchily outlined in Chapter 9 but much more needs to be filled in which the limitation of space have not allowed on this occasion. Freud and Jung complement each other in this area. Some attention was paid to the opposites of "realism" and "omnipotence" in Chapter 4 and to the opposites of embodied/disembodied in Chapters 3, 5 and 6.

Of course, not everyone is aware of the essentially paradoxical nature of the I/Self in these respects. Most of the time, our "I"s are busy on one side or the other of one pair of opposites or another erecting those defences which are the very things preventing our reaching our goals. But as we grow older and wiser we see more and more of our paradoxical or self-contradictory natures.

Another way of stating the paradoxes of the self is in terms of the location of "I"-feeling in the total personality, as the example of the robber/ant illustrated in the previous two chapters. The "I" can wander around one's Self in the same way as a traveller can wander around an allegorical or dream landscape. The gateways, obstacles, roads and water barriers such as rivers of our dreams represent movements, transitions and obstacles to the movement of the "I" about and around the Self, from one I-location or role to another. Those obstacles etc. are also observable as the blocks found by the neo-Reichians in the bodily functions and the "body armour". I have indicated that the Great Mother, the landscape mother, so to speak, is the body-image as experienced from the standpoint of an "I" which is wandering about within it, within the body-world scheme of affective experience which may be the basis of the experience of the Self. The "I" and the "self" are overlapping concepts or, rather, experiences, and in my submission have to be regarded as special sub-personalities as defined in this book, in exactly the sense in which Jung spoke of the ego-complex. The views of various authors on the origin in development of the self and of personal identity were considered very briefly in the chapter on terminology. I am an analyst of adults, not of children, nor an expert in the scientific observation of infants and mothers, and my notion of the archaic self is based on personal "memories", and the regressive behaviour and fantasies of oneself and one's adult analysands. The creation myths of the various cultures probably give the best guide to the development of the selves of the people of those respective cultures, in a practical clinical sense and as a practical way of approaching the layers of the self in an individual. Looking at the beginning of the "I" and of awareness in terms of a differentiation between light and darkness, as in the first chapter of the Book of Genesis, and looking at all the details of the various creation myths, it seems to me that we get a more practical, more dynamic and more experiential account of the archaic stages of the self than is obtained through looking at infants in a detached, behaviouristic way. Most of all, the material of one's analysands, when they are going through neurotic and psychotic phases or regressions, enables one to build one's own rough-and-ready creation myth, which has to be adapted and modified for each person and by each person. In the understanding of individual selves, there is much wisdom not only in psychoanalytic theories of development – Freud, Klein, Winnicott and now Kohut – but also for example in Jung's awesome alchemical studies and Neumann's "developmental" way of classifying myths.

This having been said, it remains true that the first major step in understanding a person's view of himself and feelings about himself is usually taken when one understands his parents' perception of him and his family's view of him. Often the self-image is a palpably direct reflection of this family view, but sometimes it is not clear which is cause and which effect. The clinical aspects of self-image and self-valuation have not been the subject of this book; they are only mentioned here in case it were thought that the psychology of the self is to be understood simply by reading the authors I have just mentioned. Each author has his own axe to grind, his own thesis to develop, and the present book is no exception.

The basic feeling of unity and continuity and of being a person is subject to marked fluctuations and disruptions in the course of analysis and other meaningful relationships. At a certain stage in an analysis a patient may feel himself not a person and have no feeling of self when separated from the therapist for longer than a short time, and the analyst may also cease to exist as a person inside the patient at the same time. Most of us are familiar with some such changes in ourselves in connection with important relationships. It is inconceivable to me therefore that any notion of self can be entertained that does not include relationship as a central consideration. The broken-up self or the non-existent self in such situations is not *really* broken up or non-existent. It is simply not present in present consciousness, and can usually be recovered immediately when the person who has been entrusted with the holding and the relating comes back again. The evidence that the self-feeling and the self-image are built up through relationships is overwhelming to my mind but certainly has not been presented in this book, so whether we regard the self as more importantly archetypal or more importantly a sort of complex has been left open. One cannot introject elements outside one's repertoire of possibilities in any case, as I have said before.

All of which brings us back to Pooh and Rabbit.

References

Allport, G. W. (1955). "Becoming: Basic Considerations for a Psychology of Personality", New Haven, Yale University Press.

Bartlett, F. C. (1932). "Remembering: A Study in Experimental and Social Psychology", Cambridge, Cambridge University Press.

Bollas, C. (1982). On the relation to the self as an object. *Int. J. Psycho-anal.* **63**, 347–360.

Cooley, C. H. (1912). "Human Nature and the Social Order", New York, Scribners.

Davidson, D. (1965). A problem of identity in relation to an image of a damaged mother. *J. analyt. Psychol.* **10**, 67–76.

Davidson, D. (1979). Playing and the growth of imagination. *J. analyt. Psychol.* **24**, 31–43.

Ellenberger, H. F. (1970). "The Discovery of the Unconscious", London, Allen Lane, The Penguin Press.

Erikson, E. (1950). "Childhood and Society", New York, Norton.

Evans-Wentz, W. Y. (1958). "Tibetan Yoga and Secret Doctrines", London, Oxford University Press.

Fordham, M. (1957). "New Developments in Analytical Psychology", London, Routledge and Kegan Paul.

Fordham, M. (1969). "Children as Individuals", London, Hodder and Stoughton.

Fordham, M. (1974). Defences of the self, *J. analyt. Psychol.* **19**, 209.

Fordham, M. (1976). "The Self and Autism", London, Heinemann.

Fordham, M. (1979). The self as an imaginative construct. *J. analyt. Psychol.* **24**, 18–30.

Freud, A. (1946). "The Ego and the Mechanisms of Defence", New York, International Universities Press.

Freud, S. (1914). "On the history of the psycho-analytic movement". Standard Edition. Vol. 14, London, Hogarth.

Freud, S. (1914). "On narcissism". Standard Edition. Vol. 14, p. 67, London, Hogarth.

Freud, S. (1914). "From the history of an infantile neurosis". Standard Edition. Vol. 17, p. 29, London, Hogarth.

Freud, S. (1923). "The ego and the id". Standard Edition. Vol. 19, p. 12, London, Hogarth.

Freud, S. (1936). "Inhibitions, Symptoms, and Anxiety", London, Hogarth.

Gordon, B. L. (1960). "Mediaeval and Renaissance Medicine", London, Peter Owen.

Gordon, R. (1965). The concept of projective identification: an evaluation. *J. analyt. Psychol.* **10** 127–150.

Gordon, R. (1967). Symbols: contents and process. *J. analyt. Psychol.* **12**, 23–24.

Gordon, R. (1980). Narcissism and the self; who am I that I love? *J. analyt. Psychol.* **25**, 247.

Gowers, W. R. (1901). "Epilepsy and Other Chronic Convulsive States" (2nd edn.), London, Churchill.
Guthrie, D. (1958). "A History of Medicine", London, Nelson.
Hall, J. A. (1982) Polyani and Jungian psychology: dream ego and waking ego. *J. analyt. Psychol.* **27**, 239–254.
Hartmann, H. (1950). "Comments on the psychoanalytic theory of the ego". The Psychoanalytic Study of the Child, vol. 5, pp. 74–96, New York, International Universities Press.
Hartmann, H. (1964). "Essays on Ego Psychology", London, Hogarth.
Hobson, R. F. (1961). Psychological aspects of circumcision. *J. analyt. Psychol.* **5**, 5–34.
Humbert, E. (1980). The self and narcissism. *J. analyt. Psychol.* **25**, 237–246.
Huxley, A. (1946). "The Perennial Philosophy". Chatto and Windus, London.
Jackson, M. (1963). Symbol formation and the delusional transference. *J. analyt. Psychol.* **8**, 145–159.
Jacobson, E. (1964). "The Self and the Object World", New York, International Universities Press.
James, W. (1910). "Psychology. The Briefer Course", New York, Holt.
Jung. C. G. (1904). Studies in word association. *Coll. Wks* **2**.
Jung, C. G. (1912). Symbols of transformation *Coll. Wks* **5**.
Jung, C. G. (1916). The transcendent function. *Coll. Wks* **8**.
Jung, C. G. (1920). Psychological types. *Coll. Wks* **6**.
Jung, C. G. (1928). On psychic energy. *Coll. Wks* **8**.
Jung, C. G. (1935). The Tavistock Lectures. *Coll. Wks* **18**.
Jung, C. G. (1937). Psychological factors determining human behaviour. *Coll. Wks* **8**.
Jung, C. G. (1944). Psychology and Alchemy. *Coll. Wks* **12**.
Jung, C. G. (1945). The relations between the ego and the unconscious. *Coll. Wks* **7**.
Jung, C. G. (1946). Psychology of the transference. *Coll. Wks* **16**.
Jung, C. G. (1950a). Concerning mandala symbolism. *Coll. Wks* **9**, Part I.
Jung, C. G. (1950b). Aion. *Coll. Wks* **9**, Part II.
Jung, C. G. (1951). The psychological aspects of the Kore. *Coll. Wks* **9**, Part I.
Jung, C. G. (1955/1956). Mysterium coniunctionis. *Coll. Wks* **14**.
Jung, C. G. (1957). Commentary on 'The Secret of the Golden Flower'. Alchemical studies. *Coll. Wks* **13**.
Jung, C. G. (1958). Prefatory note to The Transcendent Function, *Coll. Wks* **8**.
Jung, C. G. (1963). "Memories, Dreams, Reflections", London, Collins and Routledge and Kegan Paul.
Jung, C. G. (1964). "Man and His Symbols", London, Aldus Books.
Kaada, B. R. (1953). Temporal lobe seizures. *Electroenceph. clin. Neurophysiol.* **4**, 235–246.
Kohut, H. (1971). "The Analysis of the Self", New York, International Universities Press.
Lambert, K. (1981). Emerging consciousness. *J. analyt. Psychol.* **26**, 1–18.
Mead, G. H. (1934). "Mind, Self and Society", Chicago, University of Chicago Press.
Mettler, C. C. and Mettler, F. A. (1947). "History of Medicine", Philadelphia, Blakeston Company.
Moore, N. (1975). The transcendent function and the forming ego. *J. analyt. Psychol.* **20**, 164–182.
Neumann, E. (1954). "The Origins and History of Consciousness", New York, Pantheon.
Neumann, E. (1973). "The Child". The quotation in the text is taken from the 1976 Harper Colophon edition, Harper and Row, New York.
Newton, K. (1965). Mediation of the image of infant–mother togetherness. *J. analyt. Psychol.* **10**, 151–162.

Newton, K. (1975). Separation and pre-Oedipal guilt. *J. analyt. Psychol.* **20**, 183–193.

Newton, K. and Redfearn, J. W. T. (1977). The real mother, ego-self relations, and personal identity. *J. analyt. Psychol.* **22**, 295–315.

Penfield, W. and Jasper, H. H. (1954). "Epilepsy and the Functional Anatomy of the Brain", London, Churchill.

Plaut, A. (1959). Hungry patients: reflections on ego structure. *J. analyt. Psychol.* **4**, 161–168.

Redfearn, J. W. T. (1965). The patient's experience of his 'Mind'. *J. analyt. Psychol.* **11**, 1–20.

Redfearn, J. W. T. (1970). Bodily experience in psychotherapy. *Br. J. med. Psychol.* **43**, 301–312.

Redfearn, J. W. T. (1973). The nature of archetypal activity: the integration of spiritual and bodily experience. *J. analyt. Psychol.* **18**, 127–145.

Redfearn, J. W. T. (1974). Mandala symbols and the individuation process. *In* "Success and Failure in Analysis" (ed. Adler, G.), New York, G. P. Putnam's Sons.

Redfearn, J. W. T. (1977). The self and individuation. *J. analyt. Psychol.* **22**, 125–141.

Redfearn, J. W. T. (1978). The energy of warring and combining opposites: problems for the psychotic patient and the therapist in achieving the symbolic situation. *J. analyt. Psychol.* **23**, 231–241.

Redfearn, J. W. T. (1979). The captive, the treasure, the hero, and the 'anal' stage of development. *J. analyt. Psychol.* **24**, 185–205.

Redfearn, J. W. T. (1980). Romantic and classical views of analysis: primal relationship or working relationship? *J. analyt. Psychol.* **25**, 1–16.

Redfearn, J. W. T. (1982). When are things persons and persons things? *J. analyt. Psychol.* **27**, 215–238.

Russell, B. (1946). "History of Western Philosophy", London, Allen and Unwin.

Schilder, P. (1950). "The Image and Appearance of the Human Body", New York, International Universities Press.

Schreber, D. P. (1903). "Denkwurdigkeiten eines Nervenkranken", Leipzig, Mutze. ("Memoires of my Nervous Illness" (transl. Macalpine, I. and Hunter, R. A.), London, Dawson, 1955.)

Sigerist, H. E. (1951). "A History of Medicine" vol. 1, New York, Oxford University Press.

Singer, C. (1959). Medicine: Galen. *In* "Chambers' Encyclopaedia", London, Newnes.

Spitz, R. A. (1957). "No and Yes", New York, International Universities Press.

Strauss (1964). The archetype of separation. *In* "The Archetype" (ed. Guggenbühl-Craig, A.), Basel, New York, Karger.

Sullivan, H. S. (1953). "The Interpersonal Theory of Psychiatry", New York, Norton.

Temkin, O. (1945). "The Falling Sickness", Baltimore, Johns Hopkins Press.

Williams, M. (1963). The Poltergeist Man. *J. analyt. Psychol.* **8**, 2.

Winnicott, D. W. (1958). Transitional objects and transitional phenomena. *In* "Collected Papers", London, Tavistock.

Winnicott, D. W. (1965). "The Maturational Processes and the Facilitating Environment", London, Hogarth.

Winnicott, D. W. (1971). "Playing and Reality", London, Tavistock.

Wong, K. C. and Wu, L-T. (1932). "History of Chinese Medicine", Tientsin, Tientsin Press.

Woodroffe, J. (Arthur Avalon) (1950). "The Serpent Power", Madras, Ganesh.

Zimmer, H. (1948). "Hindu Medicine", Baltimore, Johns Hopkins Press.

Index

For Product Safety Concerns and Information please contact our EU
representative GPSR@taylorandfrancis.com
Taylor & Francis Verlag GmbH, Kaufingerstraße 24, 80331 München, Germany

www.ingramcontent.com/pod-product-compliance
Lightning Source LLC
LaVergne TN
LVHW021111300926
849160LV00009B/684

* 9 7 8 1 8 5 5 7 5 0 8 2 1 *